Gregory

Thank you so much
for your time at the
conference. Enjoy!

Light & Love,
Nancy

Caught between
heaven &
earth

*My profound encounters with God,
and the remarkable truth of our existence.*

NANCY VAN ALPHEN

BALBOA
PRESS

A DIVISION OF HAY HOUSE

Balboa Press books may be ordered through booksellers or by contacting:

Balboa Press
A Division of Hay House
1663 Liberty Drive
Bloomington, IN 47403
www.balboapress.com
1 (877) 407-4847

Print information available on the last page.

ISBN: 978-1-9822-2106-5 (sc)
ISBN: 978-1-9822-2108-9 (hc)
ISBN: 978-1-9822-2107-2 (e)

Library of Congress Control Number: 2019901116

Balboa Press rev. date: 03/26/2019

DEDICATIONS

To God, who directly intervened in my life, opening my eyes to the greater reality. I am eternally grateful for all creation and your love and guidance.

To my husband, Eric van Alphen, with whom I'm blessed to be sharing such an incredible life, and whose love, support and encouragement made this book possible. I love you and thank you from the bottom of my heart!

To my children, Bailey Gallagher, and Jasper and Danique van Alphen. You are the fulfillment of my role as a mother and have taught me countless lessons about love. Without each of you, I could not have moved on to the greater work at hand. I love you all!

To my sister, Rhonda, for always being there for me. Thank you for your undying love, support and friendship.

To my mom, Frances, for reaching out from the other side to provide me an inkling of things to come, and for having been my mother in this life.

To the rest of my immediate family: my dad, Donald; my stepmother, Linda; my brother, Don Jr.; and my sister-in-law, Joyce. Thank you for your love and laughter and the important roles you play in my life.

To my loyal little buddy, Charlie—our family's Cairn Terrier whose ears never went up, and who spent countless hours at my feet as I wrote into the night. Though you've crossed over the rainbow bridge, I will rub your tummy again one day!

To my mentor and dear friend Emily Rodavich, a catalyst on my spiritual journey. Thank you for engaging me in deep conversation and pointing me to new teachers and avenues of exploration.

To the "Dutch Bunch," my closest friends, Patricia and Michael, and Sophie and Henk—thank you for unending hours of laughter and friendship. You provide the much-needed comic relief in my life!

To all the amazing folks at IANDS (the International Association for Near-Death Studies), who took a chance on me and allowed me to share my experiences with an audience for the first time.

To all souls who have shared their NDE and STE testimonies and made me aware that I am not alone in what I experienced.

To all scientists, researchers, and medical professionals who are pioneers in spiritual matters. Thank you for working tirelessly to bridge the gap.

IT IS NOT THE STRONGEST OF THE
SPECIES THAT SURVIVES,
NOR THE MOST INTELLIGENT,
BUT THE ONE MOST RESPONSIVE TO CHANGE.

CHARLES DARWIN

CONTENTS

FOREWORD

DORIS ELIANA COHEN

I have done thousands of past life readings in my time as a clinical psychologist, healer, and intuitive. It gives me great pleasure to have conversations with people afterwards and hear feedback about how their past life information has helped to shed light on the uppermost struggles of their current lifetime. Nancy's story does exactly this. Sharing this awareness if a gift to everyone.

In *Caught Between Heaven & Earth*, we as readers enjoyed the journey of an intelligent and relatable human being. Grounded in logic, Nancy fought past her own skepticism and did not give up when the time came to do healing work. Despite the revelation of learning she had lived as the vengeful and murderous son of God's beloved King David, referred to in the Bible as "a man after God's own heart," Nancy sought understanding. She looked for common ground among different religions and information culled from others' present-day spiritual experiences, including the near-death phenomena. She weaves her findings into her own intriguing personal narrative, becoming the teller of her own story.

In Kabbalah (Jewish mysticism), the soul is born into this lifetime for two purposes: 1) *Tikkun*, meaning correction or making amends, and 2) to bring more light into this world. Just as Nancy shares the story of young Ben Breedlove at the beginning of her book, who is "adamant that the light had comforted him and brought him peace and happiness," so are we called to do the same. As with all of us, the past life story always clarifies and elucidates our purpose in our current life.

When we access past lives, the information may be too dark or overwhelming. No matter how dark that journey may be, we can always find that there is light behind the darkness – always! "All roads lead to Rome," as the saying goes – or in this case – to God. Nancy's journey is impressive and uplifting.

I am proud of Nancy for her courage in sharing her story with us that we might find light in it! It is valuable that she is open and sharing of her rapprochement to God. Nancy went in as an agnostic, and exited as a full-on believer. Kudos to Nancy for her persistence in continuing the work, in having courage and resilience, in doing it in a world too often filled with darkness. What a lesson for the rest of us!

Blessings, dear reader,
Dr. Doris Eliana Cohen, PhD

AUTHOR'S NOTE

Writing my story was easy. Writing this book was not. That's because in between telling my story, which came naturally, I wanted to share with readers the same things I learned along the way.

This posed a problem because as I wrote, my voice took on two different tones; that of "just me" telling my story as I experienced it; and that of what I'll call "professorial me." Not that I am by any means schooled in any professional manner in spirituality or religion, it's just that my writing becomes more academic than when telling my personal story. I suppose I could have referred to this voice as "teacher me," but I don't feel necessarily qualified to teach. What I'm doing is professing what I learned and so I refer to that voice as professorial.

The reason for the distinction is because there are two ways to read this book, and depending on who you are, you may choose to read it one way or the other. My personal story is the heart of the book, and if you are so intrigued you can't wait to find out what happens after each experience, I suggest you read the chapters that are purely about my encounters with the Divine. These are the chapters titled: Introduction; Angels at My Door; Witnesses; Vision of Christ; A Past Life Revealed; Mayhem in David's Kingdom (suggested); Confirmation I, The Tree; Confirmation II, Ireland; Confirmation III, The Cleveland Museum of Art; and Voice of God. It may be a little bumpy transitioning to non-sequential chapters, but you will likely feel more satisfied not being interrupted by the professorial me.

Likewise, those well-versed in spirituality may want to read only my personal story. Most of the information I discovered through research as my journey progressed will be highly familiar, and likely basic to these readers. However, I did strive to incorporate, and compare and contrast, information culled from the Bible, other religious texts (including non-Christian material), science, and NDE and STE literature in my quest for understanding, and this may give even readers familiar with the material a new perspective on it.

I could have chosen to write only about my experiences, but I especially wanted to include my research because I know that many who read my book will be touching on such topics for the first time. What I've included provides a great foundation for further study, and believe me, there is a vast amount of material available. I've included a suggested reading list at the end of this book.

Of course, reading the book straight through will give you the best picture of how my journey progressed. With each experience, I was driven to know more, and so I've put forth what I learned in the order I learned it. It too, is part of my story. My hope is that you'll be patient enough, and intrigued enough, to read every word no matter how you approach it.

Two final notes... 1) I am aware of my use of a lowercase "h" to denote "him" when speaking of God. While this may be offensive to some, I chose the literary convention over the religious convention. As you'll discover, man-made protocol, in my opinion, is not important to God, and further, I believe God encompasses all, including gender; and 2) Some names and place names have been changed.

With much appreciation and love,
Nancy

INTRODUCTION

Deep in the woods of Ephraim approximately 3,000 years ago, the long tresses of a young man became entangled in the branches of a great oak tree as he fled his king's army—his crime, an attempt to usurp the throne. As his donkey rode out from under him, he hung helplessly between Heaven and Earth until the army commander caught up to him, spearing him three times in the heart to end his life. Upon hearing the news, the king was gravely distraught—for the young man had been his much-beloved son.

The young man and I are also intricately connected. I discovered this when I unexpectedly embarked on the venture of a lifetime. Where his odyssey ended, mine began as I traversed a surreal chasm between doubt and belief, caught between Heaven and Earth.

My amazing true story brings you along on my journey just as it unfolded to me. In 2013, I had a series of spiritually transformative experiences (STEs) that started with me yelling at a God in whom I didn't really believe. To my utter amazement, God responded. He drew me closer from there, revealing *directly* to me truths about suffering, our souls, and our true identity. The messages I received are full of hope and love for all humanity.

I do not have an agenda, nor is it my aim to convert or convince you of the reality of my experiences. I believe everyone is on his or her individual path, and that all paths ultimately converge at the pinnacle of truth, which is God, Spirit, Source or whatever name one chooses to give the Divine power that infiltrates all existence.

My goal is simply to share my testimony of the miraculous events that transformed me from agnostic to believer. I encourage you to stay with me until the end of the book, as you'll find my encounters became progressively more profound. The very last one changed me forever. If my words happen to impact your journey, that is God illuminating your path. I am merely one of many instruments God is using to expedite the spiritual evolution of mankind.

CHAPTER 1

ANGELS AT MY DOOR

J ust when you think you've got it made—boom! Something happens to turn your world upside down. Life for me had never been better. Years of hard work and long hours were winding down. I'd spent much of my life in corporate jobs that measured worth in overtime hours— how much of my life I was willing to sacrifice. Leave work at five o'clock? Don't make me laugh. That would only get sideways glances and sarcastic questions feigning concern like, "Is your daughter sick?" To which I would furrow my brows and lie, hoping for sympathy, "Yes, she came home early from school today." Those kinds of jobs.

By the time my daughter, Bailey, entered her junior year in high school, I had already taken the exit ramp out of the corporate rat race. My plan was for us to spend more time together before she graduated. I'd worked her entire life, going back to the office after fewer than six weeks of maternity leave. I often had mom guilt and dreamed of unencumbered, carefree days with her. Thanks to Eric—my ever-supportive husband—I was finally able to do that, launching out on my own as a marketing consultant and dictating my own hours.

Eric was doing exceptionally well at his job, so for the first time since I was fourteen years old, I didn't have to work. I chose to start my business because—well, hard work is all I've ever known. Besides, I couldn't leave Eric forging the way alone for the entire family. I would have felt too guilty. Still, it was a great gig. I provided services only for clients who truly valued my work, although most of them seemed to have limited budgets. I guess there's a correlation, but I didn't care because I was happy. Eric was happy that I was happy. Bailey was happy that I was happy. So we were all just three happy peas in a pod. I was fulfilled and enjoying life, and certainly not looking to upend that.

Spending quality mother-daughter time with Bailey didn't work out as I'd dreamed, though. She was a teenager and preferred being with friends and the dreaded boyfriend, three years her senior. She also had

3

schoolwork, her part-time job at a pizza parlor, college entrance exams, and admissions tasks with which to contend. What little free time was left she spent in her room with her guitar and a head full of teenage angst lyrics, hammering out new songs. I realized I was too late. I backed off and stole moments when I could. At least I could attend school functions without begging for time off from work.

When not stealing moments with Bailey, I focused on my marketing projects but kept them to a minimum. I was having too much fun enjoying the previously elusive life-of-leisure, and I wanted it to last. I had freedom, I had nice clients, the bills were paid—heck, we'd even started saving for retirement. I browsed the mall again for no particular reason—something I had not done since a teenager—*and I bought stuff!* I bought new-fangled kitchen gadgets and experimented with recipes. Eric bought me a hammock swing, and I often swayed myself to sleep on the porch in the middle of the day reading the latest *New York Times* bestsellers or fluff magazines. Sometimes I slept in and went the entire day without makeup or changing out of my pajamas.

There were times I felt guilty for enjoying such freedom when nearly everyone else I knew was still laboring away. I didn't let that bother me too much though, because I knew such a luxury couldn't last—nothing ever does. So I relished every minute, certain we would hit a bump in the road and eventually I'd have to get back to the old grindstone.

That bump turned out to be more like a giant mountain dropped unexpectedly smack-dab in the middle of my comfy life. But it wasn't a financial hurdle. As I would soon discover, that mountain detoured me onto a beautiful new path of spirituality and communion with God that's changed my life forever.

It was mid-May 2013, just as dusk swept the sun below the living room window. I was home alone winding down from a busy Saturday doing errands. Lying on the couch, I perused miscellaneous articles and media on my iPad as I often did: the news of the day, followed by a link to a recipe, followed by a link to heart-healthy living advice, followed by a link to a story about a boy—a teenage boy who had recently died from a terminal heart condition known as hypertrophic cardiomyopathy (HCM). It was described as a stiffening of the walls of the heart, causing valve and blood-flow abnormalities.

The article linked to earlier YouTube videos the young man had made of himself talking about living with his condition and his impending death. He looked to be about Bailey's age and was vibrant and handsome. I couldn't help thinking *at this moment she's out with friends enjoying life, while his was tragically cut short.* I couldn't imagine the parents' grief.

Holding up hand-written note cards in the video, Ben Breedlove[1] wrote that due to his condition, he had never been allowed to play sports alongside his buddies, and he regretted missing out on that. My mind flashed to all the lacrosse, soccer, and field hockey games our kids had played in over the years, and that Eric and I had joyfully attended. I imagined for a moment how horrifying it would be if one of our children died. I was certain I'd never recover from such a loss. The thought of it turned my heart inside out. His family must have been devastated.

I'm an innately sensitive person—one who easily cries at the movies or over a dead deer on the side of the road. When I was young my parents often cautioned me to toughen up. In our society a bleeding heart is a sign of weakness, so controlling my emotions became second nature as I grew older. Something about Ben caught me off guard, though. I felt a lump in my throat and couldn't fend off tears as I watched the first of the two-part video he'd made.

When it was over, I laid my iPad on the couch and headed to the kitchen for a glass of water. As I approached the large counter peninsula that divided the living room from the kitchen, my sadness morphed into anger and I yelled and shook my fists at God, whom I'd never really acknowledged as being real.

"Why do people have to *suffer* like this?" I demanded through gritted teeth. "I just don't get why people have to *suffer*," I yelled accusingly. I made my way to the other side of the counter and rested my torso on the cold granite, my face buried in my folded arms. "*Suffering* is bullshit!" I pounded my fist on the counter. "Nobody should have to—"

A loud knock on the front door startled me. I wasn't expecting anyone and rarely did anyone show up unannounced. I wiped away the tears still on my face, walked back through the living room, and without thinking, opened the door—unusual for me as I'm generally

---

[1] https://www.youtube.com/watch?v=tmlTHfVaU9o

more cautious, especially when Eric is away on a business trip. I don't know why I was so nonchalant about opening the door, but I was.

"Hello?" I said, half intonating a question.

A robust older gentleman with white hair, a cane, and glasses stood at the door, while a heavily built older woman with a black open-knit shawl draped over her shoulders stood two steps down where the walkway met the porch. The old man peered over his spectacles—his eyes a beautiful shade of sky blue and surprisingly clear for his age—as he spoke the *only* words either would say to me, and that I will never forget:

"We just came to tell you that suffering isn't going to last forever."

My heart raced, and my mouth fell open. I looked to the woman, who was nodding in agreement. I barely noticed the gentleman handing me a small leaflet. I was lost in the surreal moment. I had just used that exact word—*suffering*—again and again in my tirade at God. It's not a word I use often, and I remember it felt odd coming out of my mouth, but it had kept coming anyway.

"Okay, thank you," I managed, dumbfounded.

There was a momentary awkwardness as they smiled and continued nodding but said nothing further.

"Well, good luck with your mission," I said, assuming they were from a local religious organization. More nodding and smiles. I closed the door slowly, giving them an opportunity to say more, but they didn't.

I strode the approximately eight-to-ten paces back to the couch, and in one continuous motion sat down and sprung up again, racing back to the door to find out to which church they belonged. An unencumbered blast of cold air rushed over me as I flung the door open, mere seconds having passed. I expected to see their backs, with them just having turned to walk away, but they were gone—utterly and completely gone.

I leaned out the door, looking up and down the short, empty street in front of our house. Nothing. Venturing onto the cold, rough concrete in my bare feet, I tiptoed down the porch stairs and followed the walkway that curved around our corner lot. I examined the street that ran perpendicular to our side yard, then scanned the entryways of surrounding houses. The neighborhood was deserted and eerily silent, though that was not too unusual. It had become, as of late, an almost empty-nester community. I scurried back to the front of the house and scanned the small street again. No one.

How completely bizarre, I thought. The man had a cane and they were both old. They couldn't have walked away that quickly. Nor was there a car in sight. The sun had not fully set and there was still plenty of light by which to see. I was stunned and tried to grasp the situation. *What just happened?* I fought the overwhelming feeling that God heard me yelling at him, and had sent angels in response. *Crazy*, I thought. *No way.*

I went back inside, leaflet still in hand, and turned it over looking for information. Nowhere was there written a name, local address, phone number, or email. In a small, yellow highlighted box, in tiny seven-point type, however, was a listing of international addresses to which one could write to request more information from—Jehovah's Witnesses. Aha! That made sense (as if I'd caught them). I spotted the even smaller web address: www.watchtower.org.

For sure it was *them*. When I was a kid my dad used to flip on a deafening security siren whenever Jehovah's Witnesses came to the front door. "Ha! That'll teach 'em," he'd laugh as they ran away, scattering literature on the lawn. "And don't come back," he'd yell after them. I guess my reaction was inherited.

Even so, I puzzled—If they were Jehovah's Witnesses, it doesn't explain the serendipitous nature of their visit. How is it they seemed to respond directly to my ranting and raving at God about suffering? How did they suddenly disappear? Why didn't they try to finagle their way into my living room and attempt to convert me, or at least invite me to their church (or "Kingdom Hall," as I later discovered they're referred to)? Logically I could not explain it, so I brushed it off.

I milled around the house a bit, fluffing pillows and emptying the dishwasher until the dazed-and-confused feeling subsided. My dry throat reminded me I'd never gotten that drink of water, so I filled a glass and settled again into my comfort zone. I lay back down on the couch and continued where I'd left off…

"This is My Story, Part II. Ben Breedlove." My surreal night wasn't over yet. This video was different from the first. In it, Ben talks about the third time he cheated death. He was at school when he had a heart attack. Emergency medical service workers arrived and tried to shock his heart into beating again. As the EMS team zapped voltage through his chest, his consciousness was transported to another dimension.

Ben found himself standing in an endless white room with no walls or ceiling. He was greeted by his favorite rapper, the style-savvy Kid Cudi[2]. They were both dressed to the nines. Cudi pointed to a mirror. Ben turned to look at himself and understood that his beauty as a human being went far beyond his boyish charm and good looks. His entire life was reflected back to him in that mirror, and he could see it was a life well-lived. He felt satisfied and proud of himself. Throughout the experience, Kid Cudi's song, "Mr. Rage" played. As the lyrics *When will the fantasy end? When will the Heaven begin?* rang out, Kid Cudi touched Ben's shoulder and indicated it was time for Ben to go back.

"I did not want to leave that place," Ben had scrawled on a notecard, shaking his head "no" for emphasis.

He apparently had more to do back on Earth. He re-entered his body, once again aware of the physical world and the resuscitation activities surrounding him.

That was December 6, 2011. Twelve days later Ben recorded the two-part video. On his last notecards, which contained his final thought-provoking message, Ben asked, "Do you believe in God or (and) angels?" He responds to his own query with a simple but powerful, "I do," the truth in his eyes piercing straight through the camera lens. He died exactly one week later on December 25, 2011—Christmas Day.

The fleeting thought I'd pushed away earlier refusing to give credence confronted me again: *Could God have sent angels to my door?*

I watched Part I of Ben's video again, this time giving it my full attention. I listened earnestly as he described the white light he encountered when near death at age four. I'd glossed over it earlier, attributing it to wishful thinking. I had focused instead on his condition, the family's sorrow, and the burden he carried at such a young age.

Ben however, was adamant that the light had comforted him and had brought him peace and happiness. I had the uncanny feeling Ben was telling me personally to *believe*. Physically, I was in my living room,

---

[2] Kid Cudi is still living as of this writing, and was alive at the time Ben saw him. Researchers into soul existence have posited that souls, like God, are omnipresent.

but I felt light-headed from all that had transpired that evening, as if I were caught up in a different realm.

It all started with heartfelt compassion for Ben and his family, and then for humanity in general as I railed against suffering. If God had sent angels in response—or even if he'd guided human witnesses to my door—my proclivity was to deny Divine intervention. But Ben reached out over space and time, imploring me to think again with his poignant question, "Do you believe in God or (and) angels?"

CHAPTER TWO

A BRIEF HISTORY

L ogically minded people would have chalked up such an occurrence to pure coincidence, and I was no different. As supernatural as the "angelic" encounter seemed, in the days that followed I convinced myself I was being flighty. I didn't believe in a spiritual realm, and I felt the same way about angels as I did about God—there was absolutely no way to prove either existed.

I'd come to this conclusion while still a child. If Santa Claus and the Easter Bunny weren't real, maybe God wasn't, either. All were associated with religion, yet nobody had ever seen any of them, at least not in my limited awareness.

As a teen my thinking went deeper (barely), and I decided I was agnostic before knowing there was a term for it. I proceeded through life cautiously and on my own terms, rather than trusting in imaginary protectors such as God or guardian angels.

It wasn't always like that, though. Up until I was about ten years old I was a "believer"; which is to say, I believed because that's what I was supposed to do. Even then, my exposure to religion had been spotty at best.

When just a baby, I was baptized for the first time. I had no say in the matter. The Catholic Church requires baptism soon after birth. If at all possible, it would have happened in drive-by fashion on the way home from the hospital. Catholics believe in the damnation of the soul if not baptized. Of course, I remember nothing of it, but I know it occurred because on the rare occasion my family visited my Aunt Phyllis and Uncle Rich, I was reminded they were my godparents. Growing up, I assumed they had a mystical ability to report to God on my behavior, which meant I had to be extra good around them. This wasn't difficult however, because my sister, brother, and I were reared with the oppressive mantra that *children are to be seen and not heard.*

This ultimately shaped my introverted personality, which I fought to overcome as I got older. I was a good, quiet and shy little girl.

I do recall seeing pictures from my baptism, particularly one in which my mom is holding me, with my aunt and uncle standing behind her and peeking lovingly at me over her left shoulder. Unfortunately, after my mom's death many years later, the big cardboard box of jumbled family photos she kept, disappeared. Any evidence of my first baptism is lost to history—although Saint Anthony's Parish might have a record somewhere.

Saint Anthony's is a big, beautiful church on the southern shore of Lake Erie in Lorain, Ohio. My mother, older sister, and I attended Mass there on holidays and the rare Sunday. Back then, Mass was delivered in an enigmatic, alternating mix of Latin and English, coupled with monastic call-and-response song. If not for the constant stand, sit, and kneel edicts, I would have slept through every service. My sister and I participated in catechism classes there too (the Catholic equivalent of Sunday school), but it was not our parents' priority to get us to the after-school program, so our attendance was short-lived.

Years after my baptism, I took my first Holy Communion—another Catholic rite of passage—at Saint Anthony's. Beyond the rusty guardrail of the back parking lot there's an immense pile of limestone rocks leading down to a pebble-studded beach. I walked beside the rail in a single-file lineup of young girls, all about six or seven years old, clad in white wedding-style dresses, veils, and shiny white patent-leather buckle shoes. It was a breezy spring day, and I recall the crisp, clean smell of lake and sky as we made our way to the church's back entrance. I made certain to keep my palms pressed firmly together in prayer, having been reprimanded in rehearsal by the nuns for being sloppy.

Despite having missed a few preparatory classes, I received Holy Communion. The body of Christ—the holy wafer—was stale and stuck to the roof of my mouth. That's about all I remember of Saint Anthony's. After my first communion our attendance at church dwindled further, and we stopped going altogether by the time I was eight years old.

The second time I was baptized was out of sheer terror. On those Sundays when not in Catholic church, my sister, brother, and I found ourselves at an entirely different kind of service with our paternal grandparents.

My grandpa was a Tennessee-bred Baptist preacher, and while soft-spoken and gentle in private, he could spew fire and brimstone with the best of them. It's no understatement to say that going to church with my grandparents was scary. People spoke in tongues, ran up and down the aisles, and often fainted.

My brother, four years my junior, often joined us, his fussiness unnoticed amidst the boisterous activity. As kids, we hid our fear of the unfamiliar with laughter. My brother expressed such exaggerated, wide-eyed looks of surprise that we couldn't contain ourselves. Our go-to move was to look down as if in prayer, hiding our giggles and red faces.

What a far cry those Baptist services were from the demure Catholic Masses. Preachers worked themselves into a frenzy, pounding the pulpit and delivering the *Word* with spit and vinegar. The overriding message was that unless I was saved and baptized, I would burn in hell. To avoid such a fiery fate—and because it pleased my grandparents, whom I loved dearly—I was baptized for a second time. Shortly afterward, my grandparents moved from Ohio to Florida, and that was that.

The third time I was baptized was just for the fun of it, literally. I was enticed by the mischievous pleasure of throwing a pie in some poor schmuck's face. Toward the end of elementary school, when I was about eleven years old, my sister's friend invited us to go to VBS at VBT (Vacation Bible school at Victory Baptist Temple). It sounded like a blast, and it was! The entire week the bus driver picked us up right at our house, so there was no excuse for absences. Though VBT was Baptist, the preacher reined in his oratories, keeping them short and sweet before our day of activities began. It was *vacation* Bible school after all, and we were just kids.

Throughout the week teams were pitted against each other in games like tug-of-war, water balloon fights, and Bible trivia. We competed to earn points for "the big prize"—whatever that was, I don't recall. Getting baptized was worth big points, with the added thrill of throwing a pie in the face of an opposing team's older teen group leader. None of us were exactly keen to stand in front of the others and get dunked underwater wearing only a robe and underwear, though.

Being slightly behind, I decided to get baptized and take one for the team. I was cautioned to do it for the right reasons, but I saw no harm in it. I thought Christ might even be pleased with my willingness to drive my team toward victory.

To my disappointment, the pie throwing was a letdown. The "pie" turned out to be nothing more than whipped cream in an old pie tin. I'd imagined ooey-gooey apple or chocolate pudding pie at the least. Vacation Bible school wrapped up the next week, and with it any further exposure to formal religion in my youth.

I didn't miss going to church. Sleeping in or watching television on a Sunday morning was way more preferable. Soon enough, I was consumed with all things important to my teenage self: school, chores, friends, worrying about my looks and whether a boy would ever like me. My life was typical for a young girl growing up in northeast Ohio. Our family fell squarely into the middle class. We had a roof over our heads, food to eat, decent clothes, and a little extra cash for the drive-in, rolling skating, or the county fair when late summertime rolled around.

My dad was hard working, having spent much of his life as a welder at the local shipyard and later, up until his retirement, as a maintenance worker for the Ford Motor Company. It wasn't always smooth sailing at home. With a hot-blooded Italian mother and southern-bred father, tempers flared. There was a lot of yelling and arguing going on in our house, and getting in trouble meant a few good whacks with the belt. We were disciplined, but loved. I knew other kids who had it much worse, so I always felt grateful.

In fact, giving thanks was part of my nightly ritual. I'm not sure anyone else in my family prayed before going to sleep. It wasn't something we were taught or expected to do. It was a small habit retained from my early years of attending church. My prayers themselves were habitual as well, and lacked earnestness. I asked God to bless my family and friends, thanked him for what I had, and occasionally asked for something special—like the microscope kit I'd seen at the Hills Department Store. I had been awed to discover in a science class that life existed in such infinitesimal forms.

Something else stuck with me from church, too, and that was the golden rule: *"Do unto others as you would have others do unto you."* I don't remember exactly when or why, but at some point I adopted it as my de facto way of living. I realize now that many people latch onto it, and for good reason. What you put out seems to come back to you.

Sometime during my teen years my belief in God dropped by half. There was no tipping point, such as a tragedy or other incident that changed my thinking, but more a simple side effect of growing up. New realizations tore at the fabric of my religion, limited as that was. I encountered students in school who were of different backgrounds and faiths, I learned about the theory of evolution, and heard (likely from television and other common sources) about the Bible's questionable history and manipulation for purposes of power and greed. It's not that anything alone had a hard and fast impact on me, it was simply that truth was getting harder to discern. I came to the conclusion that knowing anything beyond physical reality was impossible.

My foundational belief became that *there is no way to know the truth about whether or not God exists*. It was a fifty-fifty coin toss. My theology cemented itself in a stroke of swift and final justice. I didn't think about it for long, maybe a day or two, perhaps it was on my mind for a week, but once I'd made a decision, I stuck with it and didn't look back.

With my tightly-packed agnosticism and golden rule, I made my way into adulthood. Two months after graduation I married my first husband, my high school sweetheart. I was eighteen, he was twenty-three and an atheist. He was kind and smart, and we began our young married life in Connecticut, where he attended Yale University.

College was not an option for me, as my father pointed out the first day I entered high school. It wasn't in the budget. Instead, I went to vocational school during my junior and senior year of high school to learn a trade, picking up where my mother left off on her dream to become a cosmetologist. I cut, dyed, and permed hair at Glemby's Style Salon in the Higbee's Department Store at the local mall.

When first married, I cut hair at Phil's Barber Shop in New Haven, Connecticut for two years until we made our way back to Ohio, where I attended Lorain County Community College to search for my own dream. I was encouraged by a journalism professor to pursue writing, and became editor of the college newspaper, followed a short time later by a real job as a copy editor for the local daily newspaper, *The Chronicle Telegram.*

Despite my first husband's atheism, he never tried to convince me that his beliefs were right. He only shared his reasoning if we found ourselves in a perchance conversation on such matters. I skewed more toward atheism of my own volition. I'd say the ratio slipped to ninety percent against God, and a slim ten percent chance in his favor. Still, it wasn't something I thought much about; in my opinion it was a waste of time because God—and, by association, anything of a spiritual nature—simply couldn't be proven.

At odds with my agnosticism was nightly prayer. By this time, however, I reasoned that it was more a form of meditation. It was a way to release my concerns to the universe and get them off my chest. It was a way to have a modicum of power over that which I felt powerless to control. I still addressed my prayers to God, but more like one would address a fictitious friend in a diary.

Life continued to ebb and flow. After graduation from community college, I pursued my education further at the prompting of the same professor who encouraged me to write. Though burned out on writing, I continued my studies in another area that interested me, receiving a bachelor's degree with a major in anthropology from Oberlin College. My emphasis was cultural studies; researching and analyzing diverse groups within our world. The curriculum included classes in archeology, which rightly falls under the study of cultures, but those of early man long-buried in the dirt and annals of time. I spent long hours studying the origin of our species: the climb from *Australopithecus afarensis* to *Homo erectus*, and finally *Homo sapiens*—that's us, modern man. I spent a winter term at The Cleveland Museum of Natural History measuring human and primate bones, contributing to research on our long-lost ancestor and missing link, *Lucy.* Evolution was a given in my course of study, and I was a die-hard proponent. It's hard to dispute cold, hard facts and rock-hard fossils. Despite the evidence, I still allowed God his ten percent. It was clear to me even then that evolutionism is purely materialistic science.

Though I never found—or, more accurately, formulated—my dream, I was content to finish college and begin a career. Like many students, I didn't end up working in my field. Anthropology is a science for which there is little demand and limited pay. I gravitated toward marketing instead, certain I could make sense of my background to potential employers: understanding cultural influences *(developing marketing strategies)* that drive a group *(market segment)* to take action *(buy a product)* is instrumental to the job. I landed my first professional stint at an advertising agency two months out of school. In hindsight, and with many years and campaigns behind me, I actually *can* attribute much of my marketing success to my background in cultural studies.

For the next twelve years I was happy climbing the corporate ladder and enjoying married life, until things changed dramatically at home. On one hand, I was overjoyed to learn I was pregnant. On the other, divorce seemed inevitable. My then-husband was dealing with issues which I was too young and uninformed to understand. In retrospect, I believe his atheism contributed to his underlying depression, which made the problems that much harder to extinguish. In the end, my confidence—and our marriage—was shattered.

It's usually in times of trouble that people turn to God—even agnostics and atheists if backed far enough into a corner. But I never did, priding myself on holding it all together: the finances, my job, my sanity, and being a new mother. Strangely though, I caught a tiny glimpse of God shining through the darkness.

That light was my precious baby girl, Bailey. She was born on a snowy day in February, three days earlier than her scheduled Valentine's Day arrival, and four months before her father and I began living separately. She had smooth pink skin, big, beautiful dark brown eyes and a mass of thick, black hair that elicited gasps from those in the recovery room when I removed her tiny, red knit cap for the first time. From the get-go she was exceptionally good and rarely cried. I felt she instinctively knew that my life, apart from her, was fractured. She happily entertained herself with busy toys attached to her crib or playpen while I readied myself for work each morning. She never fussed when I left her with a sitter. I can't remember her ever being sick. I couldn't imagine what it was like for other mothers who had issues with sleep or childcare, and I wondered how I'd gotten so lucky.

Unfortunately, evenings went quickly. After a short playtime, was feeding and a bath, then packing up the diaper bag for the next day, spent alternately at grandma's house or with the babysitter. After a few stories, I rocked her to sleep and sung lullabies as she studied my face with her hand, gazing into my eyes until the sandman lulled her away. I was often overwhelmed with joy during those times, despite the turbulence of divorce. I couldn't help but thank God for her, the feeling was so beyond anything I'd ever felt.

For four years, it was just me and Bay. Her grandparents helped occasionally with babysitting, and her father saw her during visits with her paternal grandparents, but essentially it was the two of us. Life was happy, but hectic; money was tight, I worked long hours, and we moved at least once a year. But I loved being a mother and I spent as much time with my little girl as possible.

From spring into late fall, I rode her in the baby seat on my bicycle or took her for long walks in her stroller. As she grew into a toddler, her hair twisted into long, shiny black curls and she became inquisitive and eager to learn. I toted her around in her little red wagon to the zoo, the park, the science center, and her favorite, The Cleveland Museum of Natural History—the same place I'd spent countless hours in a bone closet for a winter term project while attending Oberlin College. Bailey was more interested in dinosaurs though, and by four years old she could identify all the species in the museum and in her numerous dinosaur books.

To the dismay of my family, however, I did not take her to church. My mother, still a practicing Catholic on holidays, was nonetheless heartbroken I'd chosen not to have Bailey baptized at Saint Anthony's or anywhere else. My opinion was that religion is something to consider when old enough to understand what one is considering. I thought about how I'd been baptized three times, and how each was meaningless to me. I preferred to let Bailey make those decisions for herself when she got older.

In time, I met Eric. We clicked on every level. It was nearly perfect. The problem was that he lived 5,000 miles away on the other side of the Atlantic Ocean and he had a life in Holland. That life included a wife, two young children, family, and friends. Though he was unhappy in his marriage, being together seemed impossible for us for a million more reasons.

We tried calling it quits several times, but the pull was too great. We endured distance, divorce, custody and relocation battles, financial struggles, and immigration issues to overcome the barriers that held us back—not to mention dealing with the guilt of our moral compasses.

At least religion was never an issue. Eric was brought up Catholic, but like me, had rarely attended church. He wasn't religious or spiritual at all, but was a believer if forced to take sides.

At the height of our struggles, my mother passed away unexpectedly from a heart attack. She was only fifty-six years old. My family, friends, and co-workers attended the funeral. A week later, the same executive team that was at my side had the unenviable task of letting go me and several others due to a company restructuring. My happiness was coupled with stress and uncertainty.

Still, I remained determined and in love. Eventually, Eric and I made it through the difficulties and started our lives together. As the dust settled, we worked at creating a happy blended family, despite the distance. Both Bailey, and Eric's daughter, Danique, were five years old when Eric and I married. His son, Jasper, was eight. Though only Bailey lived with us, Eric's job took him back to Holland regularly and he saw his kids often. But we wanted more, so we vowed to bring our small family together at least twice a year. We both worked long hours and maxed out our credit cards to make that happen, taking wonderful, three-week extended family vacations together, with the children staying at our house for the remainder of the summer. We alternated Christmas holidays between the U.S. and Europe.

Eventually we caught up financially, which is when I hatched the plan to spend those last two precious years of Bailey's high school days with her before she left for college. Though that didn't work out as planned, and my life diverted onto an entirely different path, the years have sped by.

As of this writing, Bailey recently graduated magna cum laude from The Ohio State University. Jasper obtained his master's degree in architectural engineering and works full time for a well-established firm in Holland. He now owns a house and lives with his girlfriend. Danique graduated with a degree in graphic design and works part-time at a company while freelancing the rest of the week and working to establish her own company. We couldn't be more proud of them. They're smart, talented, caring young adults—but Jasper is the best of the three (as he declares whenever we pay them a group compliment. Wise guy!).

My life has not been exceptionally different from most people living in this country. I grew up in a middle class family. I know hard work. I've had my ups and downs. I've loved and lost, then loved again. I know the joys and struggles of family life. Nor do I think it's unusual in today's world to have no religious affiliation or spiritual bent. Luckily, I've been healthy both physically and mentally. I've never had a breakdown, depression, addiction, or anything similar. Exhaustion comes closest. As I've maintained, I'm a rather ordinary person who's lived an ordinary life—until, of course, God decided he wasn't content being a mere possibility.

CHAPTER THREE

WITNESSES

T he irony that my strange visitors might have been *Jehovah's* witnesses (Jehovah being the Hebrew name for God) sent from above, as opposed to *Jehovah's Witnesses* from the denominational church, was not lost on me. After my experiences, I decided to contact a Jehovah's Witness Kingdom Hall to confirm what I had already suspected—that the protocol of their door-to-door representatives called for more than making one brief statement and handing over a leaflet. This would seem especially true if a homeowner were pleasant, or at least didn't launch an attack with vile words and blaring sirens.

I searched the internet for the Kingdom Hall nearest my home in Ohio, where my angels would likely have belonged had they been of the earthly variety. As I dialed with trepidation, thoughts of the only two Jehovah's Witnesses I'd known crossed my mind.

Maggie was easily the nicest person with whom I'd ever worked. We were colleagues at a small advertising agency in Cleveland where I landed my first job out of college. Upon meeting, Maggie shook my hand with such zeal I thought someone should tell her she's overdoing the firm handshake thing. I quickly realized though, that it was just Maggie being Maggie. She did everything with purpose, and went above and beyond normal duties, including showing me the ropes. I was especially grateful for this because the company's owner was eccentric and could throw one off if not prepared.

Maggie had my back. She had the owner's ear too, and often fought for the staff to get what we needed to make our jobs easier. She was positive and upbeat, even with the most abusive clients. She unofficially managed the office and staff, but never put herself above anyone. She did more than her fair share of upkeep around our small office, regularly scouring the bathroom and washing the day's dishes left in the sink by others. I wasn't aware of Maggie's religious persuasion until another colleague gossiped to me that Jehovah's Witnesses were required to leave a place tidier than when they arrived, and that they were not allowed to accept blood transfusions. While I knew little about Jehovah's Witnesses at the time, that didn't sound any more cultish to me than other religions, and if Maggie were an example of members' attitudes and behavior, then I thought we could all learn something.

Besides, my BFF (best-friend-forever) from childhood was a Jehovah's Witness, and that never phased me—at least once we got past the fact. I met Tammy in third grade and we planned our first sleepover for Christmas break that year. I imagined we would do all the fun, traditional things my own family did at Christmastime, like bake cookies, watch *A Charlie Brown Christmas* on television, listen to Christmas music and color by the fireplace, or maybe even go caroling.

The first thing I noticed when my mom dropped me off was that the three-story old house with the inviting wrap-around porch and weathered white paint, surrounded by looming pine trees, looked suspiciously under-dressed. It was the perfect house for an old-fashioned, Walton-esque Christmas. My friend bounded out the door and greeted me with a big hug, grabbing my sleeping bag and leading me inside as I waved goodbye to my mom. Immediately I noticed the lack of festive bric-a-brac inside, too. There were no poinsettias in red or green tinfoil-wrapped pots; no fragrant pine garland around the old staircase railing; and most glaringly, the non-glare of an absent Christmas tree. My heart sank.

I asked Tammy, somewhat shocked, why they didn't have their tree up yet. At that moment she set aside her usual bubbly personality, looked at me in all seriousness and stated matter-of-factly—as I later imagined she'd practiced—that their family were Jehovah's Witnesses and didn't celebrate Christmas with all the bells and whistles. Quickly and to-the-point, she added that they still believed in God and Jesus, they were *not* Satan-worshipers, and that I shouldn't worry because we were still going to have the best weekend *e-v-e-r*. Done. Then she returned to her normal, outrageous self, certainly feeling relief that the disclosure was out of the way. My disappointment was fleeting, and we did indeed have the fun-filled, giggling, stay-up-all-night kind of weekend only BFFs could have. We went on to have many more sleepovers in the years that followed, and I never gave a second thought to Tammy's religion.

I dialed the Jehovah's Witness office expecting a friendly voice, but dreading a possible all-out conversion attempt. The hall secretary, another Tammy, picked up the phone and greeted me enthusiastically. I told her I was doing research for a book and had questions about their organization's canvassing techniques. She hesitated, fearing Jehovah's Witnesses would be cast in a negative light. I assured her that was not the case and promised to tell her at the end of our conversation more about the book and my reason for the call. I did not want to taint her answers. She seemed intrigued and at ease, obliging me with answers.

"Members always go out in groups of two or more," she started, a bit protective. "One is usually female, so women don't feel scared."

That's one for Jehovah's earthly witnesses, I thought.

"Instead of 'canvassing', we call it 'publishing', and our canvassers are called 'publishers'," she corrected. "That's because we're putting the good news of the gospel out there, kind of like publishing," she said happily. She cautioned that "end times" were near, and that Jehovah's Witnesses work to *save* as many people as possible, getting right to the point by opening conversations with the closing book of the Bible, Revelations.

"I understand getting right down to business," I interjected. "But would your canvassers, er—publishers—introduce themselves first?"

"Oh, yes," she confirmed. "They go through training and, yes, that's part of it, they *would* introduce themselves first."

Doom and gloom averted.

"Would they say they are with Jehovah's Witnesses?" I asked.

She repeated that they would introduce themselves, but might not mention the organization right away; the goal was to be invited inside for a deeper conversation. I didn't probe. We both knew admitting to being a Jehovah's Witness upfront would mean a lot of slammed doors. That's likely why the organization's name is hidden on their literature. It's either extremely tiny, only on inside pages, or posted as "JW" instead of being spelled out. Marking it too overtly would likely get it trashed immediately.

Tammy highlighted that a publisher would ask questions about one's life and whether they were experiencing difficulties, or if life seemed meaningless.

I commented that it was a heavy discussion to get into with a stranger.

"We wouldn't still be doing it this way if we didn't find people in need," she said. "Once we share the news of God's Kingdom, it gives them hope."

I steered the conversation to the less theological aspect of their approach.

"So if you get a receptive listener, you open the Bible right there at the door and teach scripture?" I asked.

"Yes, ideally we sit down and read Bible passages or our literature with those willing to listen," she replied.

"So—where do you do this?" I probed. "Right there at the door, outside?"

She chuckled at such a simple question.

"Well, if we have a receptive listener, we would ask to come inside to talk more," she said.

Bingo! "So it's common to *ask* to come inside?" I pressed.

She acknowledged that publishers are taught to suggest they step inside for evangelism, culminating in an invitation to a Kingdom Hall meeting.

"Always?" I asked.

"If we get that far," she laughed again. "If someone is interested, but doesn't have time to talk, protocol is to set up another visit."

I asked about literature and Tammy told me it all comes directly from their main organization. Nothing is written or produced by anyone other than their Ruling Council.

"Sometimes, local Kingdom Halls stamp their information on it," she added.

I told her the piece I was given was titled, "All Suffering Soon to End."

I heard her fumble with a paper, saying she didn't see it on her list.

"It's been a while since I received it," I offered.

"What does the leaflet they gave you say about suffering?" she asked.

I summarized the content and she acknowledged that it sounded correct according to her understanding.

She proceeded to run down the titles on her list, explaining each. I detected her trying to surmise my religious crisis, and we detoured into a game of twenty questions. My responses deflated her eagerness to help, and she finally gave in and simply offered to send me a small booklet titled, "What Does the Bible Really Teach?" It presented a snapshot of Jehovah's Witnesses' beliefs and tenets.

I happily accepted, considering it yet another piece to fit into the bigger spiritual puzzle I was putting together. I then steered the conversation back onto my intended course.

"So if your literature isn't guaranteed to have local information on it, how would someone know where to go or whom to call with questions?" I asked.

"Most of our people have cards—like business or calling cards," she answered.

I hadn't thought about that.

"Or they just write the information out for you," she added.

In my head, I checked off everything I hadn't received: a business card, an invitation to a Kingdom Hall meeting, a request to come inside to talk, a solicitation for a future visit, not even a personal introduction. With that I tried to end the call, more certain than ever my heavenly visitors had been just that.

Tammy reminded me I hadn't shared my story yet, so I told her all about the witnesses that showed up on my doorstep. She was surprised by the lack of interaction.

"That's *all* they said?" she asked.

"That's it," I said, repeating the old man's phrase: "*We just came to tell you that suffering isn't going to last forever.*"

She drew out her next sentence, "Sure doesn't sound like something our publishers would do. And disappearing like that and all, that's so strange," she said.

"That's why I think they were actually *angels.*" I laid it on her, maybe a little too thick.

She tripped over her words, "Well angels are—. In the Bible they tell us—. There's the archangel Michael."

"It's okay," I told her. "I'm not looking for answers about angels, just how Jehovah's Witnesses go about their door-to-door activity."

By then an hour had passed, but Tammy didn't let me off the hook that easy. Before hanging up, she made me promise to call again when I felt confused or hopeless.

Chapter Four

Suffering

W hen I received Tammy's booklet in the mail I compared the chapter on suffering to the leaflet my angels had given me. Both pointed out that in the beginning, God parented man:

> I, Jehovah, am your God, the One teaching you to benefit yourself, the One causing you to tread in the way in which you should walk. (Isaiah 48:17)

In both versions, God's sovereignty is challenged. However, that is where the similarity ends. The most significant difference is that in the *booklet*, Satan is the instigator. He challenges God's right to rule, then convinces Adam and Eve to follow his lead. The *leaflet* makes no mention of Satan at all; it is man who seeks to rule himself and, of his own free will, walks away from God.

Such a glaring discrepancy gives me further reason to believe my angelic visitors were of a higher nature. When I researched the activities of angels on earth, I discovered they often utilize physical objects in their assignments assisting humans. In my case, it seems they plucked an existing leaflet out of time. The leaflet given to me was copyrighted 2005 and was out of circulation when it was given to me in 2013. By then, the responsibility for the cause of suffering (as put forth in Jehovah's Witness literature) had changed from man to Satan. I believe my heavenly visitors provided me with an old brochure because it had the correct information; that man, not Satan, is responsible for our own fall.

In both versions, God, having granted man free will, steps aside. According to the leaflet I was given, this is when man's tragic experiment commences. Humans' political, social, economic, and religious systems prove dismal. God is no longer involved and thus no longer sustains human bodies in perfection, leading to aging and death. Consistent with the laws of genetics, the offspring of Adam and Eve for all future generations inherit this *dis-ease*. Suffering ensues.

Judging from a present-day vantage point, humans have certainly lived up to their inability to govern themselves. Poverty, hunger, sickness, violence and crime have plagued humans from the beginning of civilization and no one knows how to end it. Even debating it causes more strife. Nor are we anywhere close to eradicating death. The probability of wiping out suffering on our own is nil.

I looked to other sources for a cursory comparison of suffering. The Genesis story of man is closer to that in the booklet Tammy sent than in the leaflet given to me by my angels. It tells how Lucifer (aka, Satan) challenged God, then tempted Eve to eat the fruit of the tree of knowledge, which God had forbade. Once Adam and Eve disobeyed God's rule, sin, suffering, and death ensued. It was man's choice to distance himself from God by disobeying him, and all born of man would inherit Adam's sinful nature and suffering.

There are numerous interpretations of the fall-of-man passages in the Bible, but that is the basic story. Details aside, humans clearly suffer—and not a little. Our lives are imbued with both physical and mental suffering; we endure it personally and in our compassion for others.

I probed further to see where Jesus' suffering fit into this picture, and the claim that it would abolish ours. My angels had told me that suffering would end, but they never told me *how!*

Not surprisingly, I found many interpretations of Jesus's mission. I looked for what Jesus himself had to say, though there are few quotes attributed directly to him. What little he does reveal however, is telling:

> And his disciples asked him, saying, "Master, who did sin, this man, or his parents, that he was born blind?" Jesus answered, "Neither hath this man sinned, nor his parents: but that the works of God should be made manifest in him." (John 9:2-4 KJV)

Whoa—Jesus says that neither the man nor his parents have sinned. Nor is the man's blindness a result of sin. This is a glaring departure from the idea that sin is passed down from generation to generation, and that suffering is a result of sin. Of course, the man and his parents were not perfect, but were they sinners?

In another passage, Jesus says no one sin is greater than another, if those in question are in fact sinners:

> There were present at that season some that told him of the Galilaeans, whose blood Pilate had mingled with their sacrifices. And Jesus answering said unto them, "Suppose ye that these Galilaeans were sinners above all the Galilaeans, because they suffered such things? I tell you, nay: but, except ye repent, ye shall all likewise perish. Or those eighteen, upon whom the tower in Siloam fell, and slew them, think ye that they were sinners above all men that dwelt in Jerusalem? I tell you, nay: but, except ye repent, ye shall all likewise perish." (Luke 13:1-5)

The Galilaeans are not referred to as sinners, except in the sense that those doing the questioning *presume* the Galilaeans to be sinners. Though they might have sinned, their sins were no lesser or greater than the sins of any other. This brings the present-day saying to mind, "Just because someone does a bad thing does not make them a bad person." If we are not by our *true* nature sinners (we are created in the image of God, after all), and the blind man in John 9:2-4 is not suffering because of sin, are sin and suffering truly related beyond the initial cause (the separation or "fall")? As with the blind man, maybe God's grace and good works will be made manifest in *all of us.*

"Repent for your sins!" is a cry I had heard often at my grandpa's Baptist church. Repenting, I was told, would "wash away my sins" in the blood of Christ, and one day, I would suffer no more. I became curious as to why my angels had not mentioned that I needed to repent. They told me factually that suffering wasn't going to last forever. The blind man did not repent, either, before he was healed. I felt confused and looked to decipher the meaning of "repent" further:

The definition of *repent* is as follows:

1) To feel sorry, reproachful, or contrite for past conduct; to regret or be conscience-stricken about a past action, attitude, etc.

2) To feel such sorrow for sin or fault as to be disposed to change one's life for the better; to be penitent. (Dictionary.com)

A look at the word origin supports this secular definition:

> c.1300, "to feel such regret for sins or crimes as produces amendment of life," from Old French repentir (11c), from re-, here probably an intensive prefix (see re-), + Vulgar Latin *penitire "to regret, "from Latin poenitire "make sorry," from poena (see penal). (Dictionary.com)

Further, the two words have diverged over time:

> The distinction between regret (q.v.) and repent is made in many modern languages, but the differentiation is not present in older periods.

Could it be that God, seeing us first as his perfect creation and our nature as sin-free, is using suffering as a teaching opportunity to improve our individual conditions, similar as he did with the blind man? Perhaps the way for humanity to be collectively saved from suffering *is* through repentance, which simply means to individually recognize and have remorse for wrongdoings, and work to change one's self for the better. This diminishes the suffering we cause others. As they do the same, suffering gradually comes to an end.

God undoubtedly has a plan and a purpose. It's a widely held Christian belief that God knew man would fall when he created us with free will. Much like a human familial unit, God knew his children would require lessons to grow and evolve. He could have made us dutiful, loving, and complete with all knowledge, but that goes against the gift of free will…and love given freely. We must choose these things for ourselves. Therefore, learning is offered, and for learning, a teacher is ideal.

Enter Jesus, sent to show us the way—the way to use suffering to our advantage, which is the way back to God. He demonstrated that every ounce of suffering carries the opportunity to express love, which is what we must strive for in our afflictions.

It seems that suffering has been reconfigured from something caused by the separation of man from God, to a learning tool to help us make our way back. When we return home, like the long-lost prodigal son, all suffering will finally end. Even better news—driven home to me by the teacher himself—is that suffering will end for *everyone!*

> In everything give thanks: for this is the will of God in Christ Jesus concerning you. (1 Thess. 5:18)

A Note on Religion

I did read the Jehovah's Witness literature that was sent to me. But that's not unusual considering that in the years following my STEs, I've been reading and studying everything religious and spiritual I can find. I don't believe or agree with it all, but in contrast to my agnostic days, instead of throwing everything out, I throw everything in to see what sticks based on commonalities among all belief systems and my own experiences, of course.

Where religion is concerned, I don't believe God expects us to have all the answers while we're living within a body with a brain—and ego—designed to question everything. That's why tolerance is so important. It is pure arrogance to think any single religion or person has all the right answers. Unfortunately, humans have a bad habit of condemning others who don't believe as they do.

Religion is useful in bringing like-minded souls together to study our existence and express gratitude for life and the gifts it brings. Whether this points to a creator or not isn't what's important. Even if one doesn't believe in a creator at all, it's a starting point. It's in *each other* that we find value, and whether we recognize it or not, it is God we see in each individual. This makes community ideal for getting to know God—not necessary, but ideal. Whenever two or more are gathered in his name, there is love.

Being with others who share the same beliefs is helpful in moving us forward in our spiritual evolution. No one religion is right or wrong; they're simply different paths meant for different people on different legs of their journeys. God moves each of us along at the perfect pace, and we're exactly where we need to be to achieve growth. Eventually, whether we find God through religion or on our own, we *all* arrive at the pinnacle of truth where God resides.

Howard Storm[3], self-described as a previous curmudgeon of an art professor, uncaring toward others, and an atheist, recalls in his

---

[3] Storm, Howard. *My Descent into Death. A Second Chance at Life.* New York: Doubleday, 2005.

testimony of having died and gone to Heaven (he was later resuscitated), a conversation between himself and Jesus:

Howard asks Jesus, "What is the *right* religion?"

To which Jesus answers, "The one that brings you closest to God."

CHAPTER FIVE

AN EXAMINATION OF ANGELS

F or two weeks after my experience, I was intensely focused on angels. Logically, I didn't believe in them, but I couldn't deny the extraordinary circumstances of my encounter. My good friend Emily Rodavich would call my experiences *mystical interludes*[4], a term she coined in her book of the same title. These are seemingly coincidental events with a spiritual bent, though most people don't recognize them as being divine in nature. My brush with angels was so striking however, that I couldn't help being dumbfounded both during and after their visit. I had to know more.

I searched "angels" on the internet with the intent of learning about them first from a traditional biblical perspective. Google returned a mixed bag of listings: *Los Angeles Angels Baseball, Victoria's Secret Angels Lingerie Models, Angels Daycare, Caring Angels Hospice, etc., etc.* My own disbelief aside, I was indignant God's angels didn't warrant the entire first page of internet real estate. I wondered hypocritically what the world was coming to, then narrowed the search field to "angels in the Bible," leading to several sites that enabled me to easily search biblical content. I utilized BibleGateway.com, selecting the New International Version (NIV) as my resource. These passages provide insight into angels' comings and goings:

> Do not forget to show hospitality to strangers, for by so doing some people have shown hospitality to angels without knowing it. (Heb. 13:2)

> Now when Joshua was near Jericho, he looked up and saw a man standing in front of him with a drawn sword in his hand. Joshua went up to him and asked, "Are you for us or for our enemies?" "Neither," he replied, "but as commander of the army of the Lord I have now come." Then Joshua fell facedown

---

[4] Rodavich, Emily. *Mystical Interludes*. Boca Raton, FL: Citrine Publishing, 2016.

to the ground in reverence, and asked him, "What message does my Lord have for his servant?" (Josh. 5:13-14)

In the sixth month of Elizabeth's pregnancy, God sent the angel Gabriel to Nazareth, a town in Galilee, to a virgin pledged to be married to a man named Joseph, a descendant of David. The virgin's name was Mary. The angel went to her and said, "Greetings, you who are highly favored! The Lord is with you." Mary was greatly troubled at his words and wondered what kind of greeting this might be. But the angel said to her, "Do not be afraid, Mary; you have found favor with God. (Luke 1:26-30)

Then an angel of the Lord appeared to him, standing at the right side of the altar of incense. When Zechariah saw him, he was startled and was gripped with fear. But the angel said to him: "Do not be afraid, Zechariah; your prayer has been heard. Your wife Elizabeth will bear you a son, and you are to call him John. (Luke 1:11-13)

But after he had considered this, an angel of the Lord appeared to him in a dream and said, "Joseph son of David, do not be afraid to take Mary home as your wife, because what is conceived in her is from the Holy Spirit. (Matt. 1:20)

But when they looked up, they saw that the stone, which was very large, had been rolled away. As they entered the tomb, they saw a young man dressed in a white robe sitting on the right side, and they were alarmed. "Don't be alarmed," he said. "You are looking for Jesus the Nazarene, who was crucified. He has risen! He is not here. See the place where they laid him. But go, tell his disciples and Peter, 'He is going ahead of you into Galilee. There you will see him, just as he told you.'" (Mark 16:4-7)

Angels can and do appear in human form, both in dreams and in waking life. Their main function, it seems, is to deliver messages from God, which are generally hopeful and often involve foretelling the future.

Yes! My angels passed muster, falling within the norms of angeldom—they appeared human, visited me in real time while I was awake, and had delivered the most hopeful message I could ever have imagined: "*Suffering isn't going to last forever.*"

As for the nature of angels, there is debate over whether they are a unique type of being or kindred human souls living in spirit form. An angel might be a soul that has or has not lived an incarnate life as a human (or other form). This thought is reflected societally when people say, "She's one of God's angels now," or "God needed another angel." The term "angel" in both Hebrew and Greek means "messenger." It is not a designation for another type of being. Some have argued that in Genesis' creation story there is nothing that sets angels apart from man, and throughout the Bible angels are often referred to as "men" (bolding is mine):

> While I was still in prayer, Gabriel, the **man** I had seen in the earlier vision, came to me in swift flight about the time of the evening sacrifice. (Dan. 9:21)

> A certain man of Zorah, named Manoah, from the clan of the Danites, had a wife who was childless, unable to give birth. The **angel** of the Lord appeared to her and said, "You are barren and childless, but you are going to become pregnant and give birth to a son. Then the woman went to her husband and told him, "A **man** of God came to me. He looked like an **angel** of God, very awesome. I didn't ask him where he came from, and he didn't tell me his name. Manoah got up and followed his wife. When he came to the **man**, he said, "Are you the **man** who talked to my wife?" "I am," he said. (Judg. 13:2-3, 13:6, 13:11)

Note that in the above passage, the angel does not correct Manoah for calling him a man.

> Then the **man** standing among the myrtle trees explained, "They are the ones the Lord has sent to go throughout the Earth." And they reported to the **angel** of the Lord who was standing among the myrtle trees, "We have gone throughout the Earth and found the whole world at rest and in peace." (Zech. 1:10-11)

> When they looked up, they saw that the stone had been rolled away. It was a very large stone. As they went into the tomb, they saw a young **man**. He was dressed in a white robe and sat on the right side. They were panic-stricken. The young **man** said to them, "Don't panic! You're looking for Jesus from Nazareth, who was crucified. He has been brought back to life. He's not here. Look at the place where they laid him." (Mark 16:4-6)

Angels portrayed in the following passages also appear human, but their description includes having a luminous quality (bolding mine). Could that explain the sparkle in my angelic gentleman's eyes?

> And there were shepherds living out in the fields nearby, keeping watch over their flocks at night. An angel of the Lord appeared to them, and **the glory of the Lord shone around them**, and they were terrified. But the angel said to them, "Do not be afraid. I bring you good news that will cause great joy for all the people." (Luke 2:8-10)

> While they were wondering about this, suddenly two men in clothes that **gleamed like lightning** stood beside them. In their fright the women bowed down with their faces to the ground, but the men said to them, "Why do you look for the living among the dead?" (Luke 24:4-5)

> There was a violent earthquake, for an angel of the Lord came down from Heaven and, going to the tomb, rolled back the stone and sat on it. [3] His appearance was **like lightning**, and his clothes were **white as snow**. The guards were so afraid of him that they shook and became like dead men. The angel said to the women, "Do not be afraid, for I know that you are looking for Jesus, who was crucified." (Matthew 28:2-5)

Considering the nature of angels is never fully explained in the Bible, and the portrayal of them throughout scripture is akin to man, it's plausible they are kindred souls to human beings. This idea is supported by instances in the Bible where man is also depicted with the ability to shine. In the Bible, Moses is said to have shone with the countenance of God when he descended Mount Sinai after receiving the Ten Commandments. Jesus himself says of man's future, "Then the righteous will shine like the sun in the kingdom of their Father." (Matt. 13:43) It's fair to assess that angels and humans may be cut from the same cloth.

My layman's study of angels through a traditional lens was a little like forcing a kid to eat dinner before dessert. I was anxious to get to present-day angel encounters, but happy I had done due diligence, which gave me a foundation on which to build. I was ready to move on to experiences more like mine, by people more like me—namely, those still alive.

I typed "present day angel encounters" into the search field, quickly weeding out a plethora of websites hawking "angel readings" for twenty bucks a pop—over the phone, no less. I automatically categorized these with cheesy psychics and gypsies who sit in doorways of buildings in big cities or beachside boardwalks, advertising tarot card and palm readings (Mind you, my view of those with true "gifts" has changed dramatically since my STEs.).

Other sites seemed more trustworthy, containing testimonials submitted by ordinary people not selling anything. I found myself drawn to those, as they rang true to my heart, which I've learned to trust more than ever throughout my spiritual journey. Thinking with the heart in conjunction with the head is truly a holistic approach to *being*. Here are some examples that piqued my interest:

> Dr. Frank Oski was on his rounds at the hospital and the day was nothing out of the ordinary. Then he saw an angel appear as bright as the sun in a dying patient's room. The angel said that life is an endless cycle of improvements and that humans are not perfect yet. She said that most people have this secret revealed to them when they die, but that handicapped children often know this and endure their problems without complaining because they know that their burdens will pass. Some of these children have even been given the challenge of teaching the rest of us how to love. Oski wrote about the experience in a major pediatric journal. He added that he is not looking to convince people of the experience, but does ask people to have an open mind. (www.beliefnet.com)

As I was exiting the highway, Nicholas dropped his pacifier. As I reached down to grab it to put it back in his mouth, I looked up and there was no stopping distance between me and the car in front of me. I kid you not—I SAW MY GUARDIAN ANGEL. For a brief minute, there appeared in front of me a golden, glowing figure with these "wings" and a gorgeous gown. And I SHOULD have hit the guy in front of me. But it felt like I hit a giant "marshmallow" or a big "fluffy pillow." And my daughter Katie saw her, too. "Mommy, did you see the angel?" she said. "You saw her, too— right?" I asked. Well—they say angels and spirits give off more energy than you can imagine. (www.AngelsLight.org, "Karen")

While on the way there (to his grandfather's funeral) my father ran out of gas on the freeway. A man pulled over and gave my dad a ride to the gas station.... The whole time my dad did not mention that my grandfather had just passed away. When they returned to my dad's car my dad thanked the man for the ride, got out and started walking toward his car with the gas can. As he was walking toward his car, he heard the man who had just given him a ride say the following to him: "Your father is with your mother and Suzanne (my cousin who passed away a couple years before) now and your parents are very proud of you." My dad was shocked at what he had just heard. (He) turned around to say something to the man—but he was gone. My father left that place knowing that my grandfather was happy where he was and in good hands with my grandmother and cousin. (www.Angelrealm.com, "Kevin")

An angel driving a car might seem absurd, but the utilization of physical objects is not uncommon, and they help angels appear human, disguising their real identity. I've read countless testimonies of angels delivering gas, food, clothing and other items to those in need. Generally, help is provided at a critical moment, and no one sees the angel approach. They leave just as suddenly, confounding their subjects by seemingly disappearing without a trace.

While angel encounters are not necessarily verifiable—aside from limited eyewitness accounts—those who have had near-death experiences (NDEs) in which they've met angels have the convincing element of confirmed clinical death to support their claims. A vast number of testimonies can be found on websites such as IANDS.org, the website for the International Association for Near-Death Studies; and NDERF.org, the website for the Near-Death Experience Research Foundation.

An impressive number of books written on NDEs detail many of these heavenly visits. The following stand out to me because angels in these stories appear on earth, interacting with people and objects in the physical world, as did my angels.

In her book, *To Heaven and Back*[5], Dr. Mary Neal describes her near-death experience that occurred when she drowned in a kayaking accident in southern Chile. Her body was pinned upside down in her kayak in an area of the river unreachable, but still visible, to others in her expedition party. Desperate and helpless they struggled with what to do, when out of nowhere, two men, who appeared to be native Chileans, retrieved Dr. Neal from her overturned kayak. Her husband and friends watched in amazement from the far shore as the natives chopped their way with machetes out of the thick brush to carry Dr. Neal away.

According to Dr. Neal, they reached a dirt road where an ambulance was waiting. It dropped her off at a tiny nearby hospital, drove away, and disappeared.

Dr. Neal's team later tried to find the two natives who had saved her. They searched every village within miles of the accident but could not locate them, and no one matched their descriptions. As for the ambulance, villagers were puzzled and said there had never been an ambulance even remotely close to the area, nor did the hospital own one. No one could figure out from where it had come. It also became apparent that no one had even called for an ambulance because there were no cell phone connections or land lines available.

This is clearly a case where angels manifested material objects, or at least re-located existing objectives from the earth plane for their use. What power must they have had to materialize machetes and an ambulance? The leaflet my Jehovah's Witnesses-in-disguise left behind would have been a piece of cake!

---

[5] Neal, Mary C., M.D. *To Heaven and Back: A Doctor's Extraordinary Account of Her Death, Heaven, Angels, and Life Again.* Colorado Springs, CO: WaterBrook Press, 2012.

Interestingly, Howard Storm was told by angels during his NDE, that in the future, humans would have the ability to manipulate energy and matter through thought—yet another indication that humans and angels may be the same type of beings.

In another example, an angel dictated a manual to a third-generation nurseryman, who says he knew nothing beyond basic tree management and only came into his position because his family owned the nursery. *The Man who Planted Trees*[6] details David Milarch's NDE and subsequent visit from an angel who leaves an amazing gift that puts Milarch in charge of saving the world's greatest trees and healing the planet. During his NDE, he was told he had to go back to fulfill a mission:

> "You have work to do," he said. Work? What kind of work? I didn't want to leave. But before I could get another word out I was back hurtling through the white tunnel with the first two angels to my bedroom. I lowered back into my body, and then they were gone. But what was the work I was supposed to do?

Several months later he was given his assignment by an angel who appeared in his bedroom:

> A soft, warm female voice said, "Get a pad and pen and go to the living room." I rose out of bed, found a legal pad and a pen, and sat nervously on the edge of my leather chair.

Milarch was angry at himself when he realized, upon waking up the next morning, that he had fallen asleep. However, to his great surprise, he found his notebook filled with instructions on why and how to clone trees.

> I stared in wonder at the words: Dying trees. Champion species. Cloning. Reforesting.... The earth's trees and forests getting sicker, weakened by pollution, drought, disease and bugs able to survive the warmer winters.

---

[6] Robbins, Jim. *The Man Who Planted Trees. A Story of Lost Groves. The Science of Trees, and a Plan to Save the Planet.* New York: Spiegel & Grau, 2015.

I was to clone the biggest, strongest, hardiest trees.... I felt like Noah, a simple man told to become a shipbuilder and a zookeeper.

Milarch and his son went on to form The Archangel Ancient Tree Archive, a non-profit organization established to collect DNA from the world's most magnificent trees. Ultimately, the goal is to restore Earth's vitality by repopulating her with these trees. Milarch continues to abide by the angelic manifesto and has become a guardian of the great trees, along with the angel who delivered the manifesto.

Whether surveying angels of the Bible, or examining their activities in modern times, one thing is certain—their role has remained consistent of that as messengers, helpers and guardians of the human race.

My angels certainly fit this mold. I was given wonderful news about suffering at a critical moment (I was yelling at God). I was also given a physical object, the leaflet explaining suffering; why it started and the fact that it will end.

It has become common knowledge within spiritual communities that beings serve in various roles on the other side. There are regular angels, guardian angels, spirit guides, archangels, and disincarnate souls busy doing all kinds of things in the afterlife. There is a consensus among these communities that all beings at their core are souls, and all *souls* serve in different capacities at different times, whether in or out of body. As you'll see in the next two chapters, this makes sense in light of the *absolutely stunning and most revelatory message* I was given.

CHAPTER SIX

VISION OF CHRIST

E ric arrived home from his business trip and I put my research on the back burner. I hadn't told him over the phone about my experience because I wanted to gauge his body language and facial expression when I told him about the encounter. He would be the first person I'd tell. Predictably, he was surprised, but supportive and respectful. He believed everything had happened as I described it, but he wasn't sure what to make of it. How could he be, when even I wasn't sure?

Not one for philosophical discussion, the conversation didn't last long and we spent the weekend in reunited bliss as was typical when he returned home from a trip. Between snoozes to catch up on his jet lag, we watched movies in bed and occasionally ventured out for a meal or a walk. After a while, I succumbed to the left-sided logic of my brain and attributed the incident to coincidence—albeit a strange and unexplainable one.

Soon I was absorbed again in the day-to-day details of life. Bailey would be graduating from high school the next year, and I turned my attention to senior year planning. I spent hours clicking through various photographers' pictures of smiling teenagers against faux backgrounds of New York City or sunny meadows, dressed in athletic gear, band uniforms or the latest fashions. Senior pictures were a big deal and I needed to book a studio. My to-do list grew as flyers came home from school. I added SAT pre-testing and college visit nights to graduation party planning and all the other things parents oversee prior to the last year of their child's high school days.

That's where my mind was when I went to sleep *that* night. I'd nearly forgotten about the angels, but God had not forgotten about me and decided we would continue our conversation.

I have no idea what time it was, but I do know I was in a deep sleep and not dreaming. I suddenly sensed someone standing near me, which caused me to awaken—not in the sense that I opened my eyes, but I became aware, as alert as when fully awake. I don't know of a word to accurately describe this state. Researchers who study spiritually transformative experiences (STEs), dreams, and visions often use the word *hypnagogic* to describe the drowsy condition between sleeping and wakefulness, but I didn't feel drowsy. My consciousness was at once fully alert, though my body remained in a sleeping position and my eyes were closed. I did not feel as if I was floating, nor did I see my own body as someone having an out-of-body experience might. I did however, feel I was *in spirit*. This is the best way I can describe it. I don't know what, if any, criteria defines a vision, but it seems appropriate to describe this second experience as just that.

When I was awakened, I saw a figure standing in the distance in front of me and slightly to the left. I recognized instantly, and was awed by, the presence of *Jesus Christ*! He was far enough away that I could see his entire body, which struck me as odd because it had felt as though he'd been standing within my personal space. He was standing in a misty area, dressed in a white robe with wispy, soft white, purple and yellow-gold streaks of light dancing and flowing over his garment. I sensed with every ounce of my being that it was Jesus. Amazingly, I realized I *knew* him!

This in itself was strange because I'd never given Jesus much thought. I viewed him only as a man who'd lived 2000 years ago, claimed to be the son of God, had some wonderful ideas about how to live, and was ultimately crucified for blasphemy. I was agnostic and had never felt compelled to learn more; Jesus' divinity couldn't be proven. It seems foreign to me now that I had ever thought that way because Jesus continues to personally guide me. My prior logic proved to be flawed and immature.

My reaction upon seeing him was complete surprise. Although I knew him, I sensed seeing him had not been part of the *plan*; whatever that was, I wasn't sure. Jesus showing up here on Earth, in my house, in my bedroom, in the middle of my life, struck me more as an unexpected pleasant surprise than that which I later attributed it to be—a miracle! I liken my reaction to seeing a dear old friend whom you hadn't thought about in ages and who lives a million miles away, in the local supermarket when you had no idea your friend was in town. As soon as I saw him, I exclaimed *"Jesus!"* just as you would shout out that old friend's name with joyful surprise.

Communication was not verbal, but through thought. I've since learned NDErs have long described communication in the spirit world in this manner, generally referred to as *telepathy*. Communication is instantaneous and transferred as entire thoughts, rather than words strung together into sentences that must be interpreted into thoughts. Telepathy eliminates miscommunication, and this is how Jesus and I communicated, though it was mostly he who did the talking.

Another element of my vision, also commonly reported among NDErs, was the rapid pace at which thought, understanding, and action occurred. This high-speed exchange set my vision apart from typical dreams. Simultaneous to me calling out Jesus's name, he moved forward—so close his head and shoulders took up my entire field of vision. He didn't walk or float, but suddenly changed location. His hair was shoulder length, light-to-medium brown in color, wavy, and parted down the middle. Jesus's face, however, was blurred out by horizontal, cloudy striations. Dark areas were apparent where his eyes, nose, and mouth would be located. I don't recall seeing anything like a beard, but I had little time to examine details.

Upon seeing his face close-up, I blurted out telepathically, "What do you look like?" For some time after my experience, I was upset with myself for asking such a superficial question. I could have said or asked anything, and I came up with "What do you look like?" In hindsight, however, I believe Jesus intended me to ask it. I received an astonishing three-part answer.

As soon as I had formulated the question, my vision was snapped to the right. I saw an endless stack of photos being riffled through like a deck of cards, the corners being released by an invisible thumb. I could clearly see pictures of people of diverse races and backgrounds. As I watched, Jesus communicated to me that he looks like all people because he is all people—we are all *one*. He did not speak these words, but dropped the entire thought into my consciousness.

The last picture fell into place on top of the pile, and then everything slowed down significantly. The picture gradually rose up, floated to the right, and hung in mid-air. I followed the photo's movement while discerning it was a picture of a father and son. They were standing next to each other, the father's arm draped around his son's shoulders and the son's arm around his father's waist. Jesus confirmed my assessment with another thought burst into my mind: *I am also the Father and the Son.* This was the second part of his three-part answer to my seemingly superficial question.

The picture remained in place for an inordinate amount of time, which puzzled me because I thought I'd already understood the message. I assumed I needed to examine the photo closer, which I did. It looked normal, and I remember thinking it was the kind of photo you might find on a fireplace mantel. The father appeared to be in his mid-forties, and the son about thirteen years old. I waited to receive another thought from Jesus, but it didn't come. Instead, the picture continued to hang in mid-air, prompting me to keep studying it.

I observed the two had genuine smiles, and they looked happy together. They also had similar body types—pleasantly plump, but not obese. They were dressed in plain, relaxed clothing, and both had straight, jet-black hair and tanned skin. It suddenly occurred to me that they looked—*Mexican!*

Upon this realization, the vision abruptly ended and I knew I'd gotten it right. This was the detail Jesus wanted me to notice. It's not that I can give an exact description of the father and son, but I suspect I will recognize them when I see them. Their images are burned somewhere into the back of my mind. While it is odd that Jesus would portray himself as being any specific nationality after he'd just told me he looks like everyone, I believe he had a specific reason for doing this. I believe the third part of the answer to the question "What do you look like?" was intended to prepare me for a time when my path will cross with the father and son in the picture, and I will be able to help them in some way or vice-versa. It seems Jesus wanted me to be aware of what I now know he was quoted as saying in Matthew 25:40: "Truly I tell you, whatever you did for one of the least of these brothers and sisters of mine, you did for me."

I later wondered how and where I would possibly meet anyone Mexican. There wasn't much of a Mexican population to speak of where I lived, short of the family who owned the Mexican restaurant in town and had become my marketing clients. I knew the entire family, and none of them were the father and son in the picture. I thought the chance of meeting more Mexican people would be slim, but I decided not to worry about it. It would happen when it was meant to happen.

Amazingly, nearly two years later Eric and I relocated for his job to southern New Jersey, where it turns out there is a large Mexican population, derived primarily from immigrants who came to work the farm fields of the rural agricultural landscape. I now routinely interact with many Mexican people.

Once my vision ended, I immediately opened my eyes. I was shocked by what had transpired. I caught my breath and leaned over to wake Eric, shaking his arm.

"I just saw Jesus," I whispered excitedly.

"What? Wow. Dat's cool," he mumbled in his sleepy Dutch accent.

I never advised him "cool" is no longer a trendy colloquialism. He shuffled under the covers and pulled them up around his neck.

"I *really* just saw Jesus," I exclaimed.

"I believe you," he responded, not mustering the excitement I had expected.

I acquiesced, "I guess I'll tell you about it in the morning."

That was the gist of our conversation, and he quickly fell back to sleep. I, on the other hand, lay there in wide-eyed disbelief, admonishing myself to *never, ever forget this was real.*

What Does Jesus Look Like?

When I share my story, people always want more specifics about what Jesus looked like. I can understand the curiosity. After all, when he appeared to me, face blurred, I immediately wanted to know what he looked like, too.

I am going to take my cue from Jesus' playbook and tell you *it does not matter*. There was a reason I did not see Jesus' face, and the message is same for all of us. He wants us to not only think of him as everyone, but to turn it around and think of everyone as him. That sounds silly to say because it seems redundant, but it's a matter of perspective. We likely don't have Jesus on our mind 24/7, and it's therefore easy to forget his spirit lives within each of us. We do, however, run into other people constantly. The habit we should consciously develop, is to look at others and see Christ within them first, no matter who they are, what they've done, or what they believe.

After the resurrection, there were three instances where Jesus did not appear physically as himself. Why did he do this? Did he want to test his disciples? In a way, yes. In addition to the specific messages he had for them, by appearing as a stranger he reinforced that even though he had physically left Earth, he always exists within each individual (compellingtruth.org/recognize-resurrected-Jesus.html):

> Jesus saith unto her, "Woman, why weepest thou? Whom seekest thou?" She, supposing him to be the gardener, saith unto him, "Sir, if thou have borne him hence, tell me where thou hast laid him, and I will take him away." Jesus saith unto her, "Mary." She turned herself, and saith unto him, "Rabboni"; which is to say, Master. (John 20:15-16)

> And it came to pass, that, while they communed together and reasoned, Jesus himself drew near, and went with them. But their eyes were holden that they should not know him.... And the one of them, whose name was Cleopas, answering said unto him, "Art thou only a stranger in Jerusalem, and hast not known the things which are come to pass there in these days...?" And it came to pass, as he sat at meat with them, he took bread, and

blessed it, and brake, and gave to them. And their eyes were opened, and they knew him; and he vanished out of their sight. And they said one to another, "Did not our heart burn within us, while he talked with us by the way, and while he opened to us the scriptures?" (Luke 24:15-16, 18, 30-32)

But when the morning was now come, Jesus stood on the shore: but the disciples knew not that it was Jesus. Then Jesus saith unto them, "Children, have ye any meat?" They answered him, "No." And he said unto them, "Cast the net on the right side of the ship, and ye shall find." They cast therefore, and now they were not able to draw it for the multitude of fishes. Therefore that disciple whom Jesus loved saith unto Peter, It is the Lord. Now when Simon Peter heard that it was the Lord, he girt his fisher's coat unto him, (for he was naked,) and did cast himself into the sea. And the other disciples came in a little ship; (for they were not far from land, but as it were two hundred cubits,) dragging the net with fishes.... Jesus saith unto them, "Come and dine." And none of the disciples durst ask him, who art thou? knowing that it was the Lord.... This is now the third time that Jesus shewed himself to his disciples, after that he was risen from the dead. (John 21:3-8, 12, 14)

Jesus taught this lesson long before the crucifixion, and long before teaching it to me directly. In the following passages, Jesus answers his disciple, Philip, when asked what God looks like, explaining our unity in the process:

Jesus answered: "Don't you know me, Philip, even after I have been among you such a long time? Anyone who has seen me has seen the Father. How can you say, 'Show us the Father'? Don't you believe that I am in the Father, and that the Father is in me? The words I say to you I do not speak on my own authority. Rather, it is the Father, living in me, who is doing his work. Believe me when I say that I am in the Father and the Father is in me; or at least believe on the evidence of the works themselves. (John 14:9-11)

Before long, the world will not see me anymore, but you will see me. Because I live, you also will live. On that day you will

realize that I am in my Father, and you are in me, and I am in
you. (John 14:19-20).

Unfortunately, as foundational as this is, many are far from learning
and living it. Only when we recognize that we are one and care for each
other as such, can we lift the whole of humanity to a higher elevation
of being.

CHAPTER SEVEN

WE ARE ONE

J esus imparted to me the truth of humanity's identity. It's not that I
had been looking for answers about it specifically, but coming on
the heels of my outburst at God about suffering, my best guess is that
Jesus graciously decided to round-out the picture of humanity for me.
Rather than suffering beings left to fend for ourselves on a lonely planet,
I learned not only that there is a reason for suffering and that it will come
to an end, but that being alone is an impossibility.

The message from Jesus is that we—God, Jesus and all of us—
are one. For a presentation board I displayed years after my STEs
at a conference on near-death studies, I showed this relationship in
Venn diagram form—three circles overlapping in the middle. It was
rudimentary, yet on par to understanding what is actually the quite
simple relationship of *separate but one*. Jesus clearly showed me that we
are all an inseparable part of God.

How did it come to be then, that humans lost sight of their identity?
One of the most glaring reasons is the early Christian church hid it from
us, prohibiting associating ourselves with God. This thinking flowed
into the mainstream and has lived on into our modern world. Whether
Christian or not, that anyone would equate themselves with God would
be seen as the pinnacle of arrogance. Society has a tendency to put
people down after all, not raise them up.

A delve into the history of Christianity, the scriptures themselves,
NDEs and STEs, and a look at recent scientific discoveries all return
the same truth Jesus told me, that we are all one.

But to say we are God—well, that's blasphemy! There was a time
I would have been executed for proposing such a thing. Jesus himself
was crucified for making this same claim. He even tried to put it in
terms humans could understand, saying he was the son of God, "son"
implying he was of the same substance as God. He also tried to make
us aware that we are all children of God, and likewise of the same

substance. Never did he make this more clear than when he said, "Ye are Gods" (John 10:34). Early Christians knew and celebrated this, but somewhere along the line it got lost.

It was Roman Emperor Augustine's pre-Christian belief in Manichaeism that drove humans and God further apart (the "fall" being the initial separation). Augustine clung to the idea that evil is separate from good, which skewed his understanding of Christianity. He demanded the church position God (good) as separate from humans (evil). Church authorities scrambled to introduce the new edict into the Christian story and a false foundation replaced truth.

The contrived idea of "ex nihilo" forced followers of Christianity to accept that God created human beings *out of nothing*. This forged a chasm between God and his children which grew wider over time. God became a distant and unrelated creator to be feared, one that doled out punishment, even annihilation, in his wrath. Though still referred to as a "father," God no longer appeared to love unconditionally. This duplicity of the nature of God has been positioned by the church as the "mystery" of God, and it continues to confound Christians to this day.

Fortunately, it is wrong. The concept of ex nihilo does not appear anywhere in the Bible. What can be found are examples to the contrary. Even after the church nixed the idea of God and his creation being as one, they did a sloppy job of hiding text that supported it (Holy Bible, KJV):

> In the beginning was the Word, and the Word was with God, and the Word was God. (John 1:1)

> In him was life; and the life was the light of men.... That was the true Light, which lighteth every man that cometh into the world. (John 1:4, 9)

> Jesus answered them, "Is it not written in your law, I said, Ye are gods?" (John 10:34)

> "I am the vine; you are the branches. If you remain in me and I in you, you will bear much fruit; apart from me you can do nothing." (John 15:5)

Genesis 1:26-27 and 9:6 indicates that man is created "in the image" of God. In 2 Corinthians 4:4 the same phrase is used to reference Jesus as being made in the "image of God." Jesus states in John 4:24 that God is spirit. Taken together, we can deduce that man was created as spirit, "in the image of God." Therefore our true nature is that of spirit, as God is also spirit. The body is secondary. As author C.S. Lewis aptly put it, "We don't have a soul. We are a soul. We happen to have a body."

Often, this argument is countered with verse in Hebrews 9:27, "And as it is appointed unto men once to die, but after this the judgment." I suggest this alludes to the body only. Additionally, as I share in later chapters, the idea of *judgment* has been misconstrued as well.

God and His Creation as Separate versus *God and His Creation as One* is a debate over which volumes have been written. Different interpretations of Bible passages, subjective histories, and so much more have been heaped onto the pile by both sides that there seems to be no end to the argument. So where is truth found? I can only suggest one recall Jesus' words in Luke 17:21 "For lo, the kingdom of God is within you." The answer is always found within. Ask, and then listen. It was during such a calm respite in my life, when a deep empathy came over me, that I made that first connection.

The phrase, "Be still and know that I am God," often comes to mind when I consider why my STEs occurred. I believe God always answers us, but because we are cut off by our ego (the part of us that believes we are separate from God), we fail to notice his responses. My friend Emily would say we're tone deaf to the mystical interludes! The real reason we fail to hear God is because we block out God with logic. Our feelings, gut instincts, intuition, whatever one chooses to call that "still, small voice," is even more important than logic, and I've learned to trust it.

It is interesting that God seems to have spoken directly to people in the past more than in present times. Could this be because we shut down the channels of communication when we bought into the idea of ex nihilo, or like many atheists and agnostics, decided God was not real or within our grasp?

Or could it be that God and Jesus are speaking to people today more than ever? Judging from the vast amount of NDEs and STEs occurring, I say the answer is a resounding *yes*. While these experiences

59

are happening to people from all walks of life, those with medical backgrounds—generally respected as followers of science—are pioneers in the new spiritual frontier. They stand at a unique vantage point between science and spirituality, and are respected enough that people will listen to their claims.

In *Dying to Wake Up*[7], Dr. Rajiv Parti, chief of anesthesiology at the Bakersfield Heart Hospital in California at the time his NDE occurred, writes about the Christ consciousness that binds all, despite his being a life-long Hindu:

> But now mine (nde) had a twist: I had been blessed to be in the presence of Jesus. I didn't know what that meant and didn't quite know what to do. At first consideration, I thought I was being asked to convert to Christianity, but as I thought further, I realized it might be something different altogether. Jesus had asked me to 'spread (the) message of universal love, of Christ consciousness.

Dr. Parti realized he was to serve all religions and the Christ consciousness common to all, which he also refers to as the "universal consciousness." He was instructed to become a consciousness-based healer, and though he had no idea how to go about it, he was assured angels would guide him.

Soon after, the angels Michael and Raphael, whom he had spoken with during his NDE, appeared and inspired the writing of his "The Near-Death Manifesto," which includes specific references to oneness:

1. Consciousness can exist outside the body.
2. There is life after death.
3. We have past lives, and our experiences therein can shape our current realities.
4. We are all connected to each other because we are all made of the one and same energy that manifests as differentiated matter.
5. Divine beings exist to help and guide us.
6. There are different levels of consciousness.

---

[7] Parti, Rajiv, M.D. *Dying to Wake Up. A Doctor's Voyage into the Afterlife and the Wisdom He Brought Back.* New York: Atria Books, 2016.

7.   There is one, all-pervading, supreme love and intelligence that is the source of the entire universe, and that love is the supreme source of creation.

Dr. Eben Alexander, author of the New York Times #1 bestseller *Proof of Heaven*[8], had been a practicing neurosurgeon for over twenty-five years at the time of his NDE, including having served fifteen years at the Brigham & Women's Hospital, Children's Hospital, and Harvard Medical School in Boston. In a 2014 interview[9], Dr. Alexander says his experience proved to him that conventional scientific theory of consciousness was wrong, though he had been a hardcore advocate of it himself. That brain creates consciousness (likened to a soul), was the exact opposite of the truth he discovered:

> So I've come to realize that consciousness, soul, or spirit is the thing that truly exists at the core of all that is. Before my coma I would have been tempted to try and tell you that, as conventional scientific teaching says, the brain, the chemistry, the biology creates an illusion of reality, an illusion of free will. In fact that is absolutely backwards. What truly exists is consciousness, soul, or spirit.

He goes on to emphasis that the consciousness he encountered at the core of his journey (which he refers to as God, or "Om," the sound he heard at the core), is that which binds all beings:

> A central message in *Proof of Heaven* is that consciousness is at the core of all existence. I think the most important aspect of that lesson, which is brought back by so many near-death experiencers and other spiritual journeyers, is that we are all eternal spiritual beings, and in fact our very consciousness is a direct link to the infinitely loving creative source at the core of

[8] Alexander, Eben, M.D. *Proof of Heaven. A Neurosurgeon's Journey into the Afterlife.* New York: Simon & Schuster, 2012.
[9] https://www.newdawnmagazine.com/articles/a-neurosurgeons-journey-to-worlds-beyond-an-interview-with-dr-eben-alexander , accessed November, 2018

all being. As so many who have had these experiences will tell you, that unconditional love is infinitely healing.

It's important for all of us to realize that we're eternal, spiritual beings, that we come back in multiple reincarnations in our ascendance toward that oneness, and that we're all in this together. Consciousness binds us all, not just as humans, not just as all life on earth – all of conscious life throughout the universe.

There are many other scientific researchers and medical professionals who have had spiritually transformative experiences, but not NDEs. They too were exposed to the same knowledge brought back by near-death experiencers.

In *Already Here*[10], Dr. Leo Galland details transcendent events around the death of his twenty-two-year old son, Christopher. Throughout, Dr. Galland struggles with his analytical mind to believe and understand the messages his deceased son gives him. In teaching his father the reason for humanity's existence, Christopher imparted knowledge about both our oneness and our "other-ness," which cannot exist without each other. Dr. Galland shares:

I've come to realize that the Singularity is now. There is no beginning and no end. No before and no after. Heaven and earth, spirit and matter, are unified opposites that together create God's moment. The universe itself is an act of overwhelming love. As Chris so emphatically explained, love exists only among separate beings. Matter is essential for separation, for the existence of the other-ness that allows love to be. That is the reason for its existence, and for ours. Through our love and caring for others, we are immersed in the divine power that creates our world.

If the universe is an act of love, consciousness is essential for existence. Our own consciousness, as individuals, is part of the Singularity. The universe exists for us to manifest love.

---

[10] Galland, Leo, M.D. *Already Here. A Doctor Discovers the Truth about Heaven.* Carlsbad, CA: Hay House, Inc., 2018.

Compassion and empathy figure greatly in the manifestation of love, which is crucial to healing, according to another pioneer in the field, Dr. Larry Dossey. In a podcast interview on *Inspire Nation*[11], Dr. Dossey talks about his latest book, *One Mind*[12], the premise of which is that consciousness is non-local. Rather than being a product born of, and unique to, individuals' brains, consciousness is infinite—meaning it exists everywhere at all times.

All individuals, Dr. Dossey says, are part of the one mind. We are essentially one being whose nature is that of love, played out in the forms of caring, compassion, empathy, protection and all else one would think of under the umbrella of love.

When one realizes the true nature of consciousness, it's easy to see the role love plays in healing. According to Dr. Dossey, patients surveyed about their medical care resoundingly state that if they could change anything, it would be that their practitioners be more caring and empathetic. Studies have proven that when medical professionals do act more loving toward their patients, healing is improved. Dr. Dossey stated that top medical universities are now instituting courses on empathy.

Dr. Dossey's exploration of consciousness was sparked at an early age by instances of what he calls "twin stuff." Like most twins, he and his identical brother often seemed to share thoughts and feelings even when distances apart. He points to quantum entanglement to illustrate how this is possible. Quantum entanglement is the phenomenon of one particle reacting to stimulation of another particle, even at great distances apart, when there is no apparent connection between the two. This basic explanation is a start to understanding the connectivity of all that exists within the one mind.

Furthering his interest, and much more shocking to him, were Dr. Dossey's pre-cognitive experiences. The first occurrence began with a vivid dream where he saw an entire surgical operation take place, which then played out the next day exactly as he had seen it. These

---

[11] https://inspirenationshow.com/inspire-399-dr-larry-dossey-one-mind/ accessed February, 2019.
[12] Dossey, Larry, M.D. *One Mind. How Our Individual Mind is Part of a Greater Consciousness and Why it Matters*. Carlsbad, CA: Hay House, Inc., 2013.

pre-cognitive dreams continued, and rather than brush them aside, Dr. Dossey embraced them as clues about the nature of consciousness.

I myself have had precognitive episodes, the most impactful a premonition of 9/11 the day before it happened (years before my STEs). Though I had a hard time dismissing it, I didn't know what to make of it and so I relegated it to the back of my mind. I've learned since that many people had premonitions of 9/11. Could it be that our one mind synced more than usual in the face of impending doom?

After many years of research, Dr. Dossey's conclusion that consciousness is infinite and foundational explains how pre-cognition is possible. If everything exists at once in the one mind, then pre-cognition is merely a matter of having accessed that information.

Bruce H. Lipton, PH.D, an internationally recognized cell biologist, reached the same conclusion about our interconnectedness but derived his evidence, not surprisingly, from cellular research. His finding is that consciousness—and more specifically, *belief*—rather than DNA, drives biology.

As it turns out, DNA is not the end-all-be-all we've been led to believe, and the famous genome mapping project started in the 1970s, turned out to dispel the hopes of science to match specific genes to specific diseases and disorders. According to Lipton, DNA is more like a blueprint that tells our new-born bodies what the antecedent structures have been like thus far—that which has been passed down from generation to generation. DNA tells our bodies, *Okay, here's the blueprint we've been using, let's use it again with minor modifications for the new structure.*

However, similar to building a house, you as the owner have the right to choose to do something completely different, and that is purely consciousness controlling matter. How our bodies work, Lipton explains in his book, *The Biology of Belief*[13], is based on the ability of trillions of individual cells to come together to form communities that work in conjunction with each other for the greater good, namely the entire body. These cells initially have no notification of their station but are assigned chemical and structural signatures to join other cells assigned

---

[13] Lipton, Bruce H., Ph.D., *The Biology of Belief. Unleashing the Power of Consciousness, Matter & Miracles.* Carlsbad, CA: Hay House, Inc., 2005.

to similar functions. Lipton takes us through the details of why DNA is not ultimately responsible for this, but that it is an unknown force controlling the assembly of these communities that make up the body (organs, tissues, etc.).

To that end, Lipton joins other scientists in pointing to quantum physics and entanglement to demonstrate that there is an unknown force controlling matter. That unknown force, Lipton concludes, is the mind—not the brain, but consciousness.

As such, belief is of paramount importance in managing our own health. If we do not believe we control our bodies, then we never take the step toward practicing "mind over matter." The more one believes, the more they master control.

Lipton provides a noteworthy example, sharing the story of physician Albert Mason, who had been experimenting with hypnosis when visited by a fifteen-year-old boy whose body was covered with warts, as diagnosed by the referring surgeon. With full confidence, Mason hypnotized the boy and after the first session, the warts completely vanished from his arm, the area Mason had targeted.

What happened next is even more revealing:

> When Mason brought the boy to the referring surgeon, who had unsuccessfully tried to help the boy with skin grafts, he (Mason) learned that he (the surgeon) had made a medical error. The surgeon's eyes were wide with astonishment when he saw the boy's arm. It was then that he told Mason that the boy was suffering, not from warts, but from a lethal genetic disease called congenital ichthyosis. By reversing the symptoms using "only" the power of the mind, Mason and the boy had accomplished what had until that time been considered impossible.

When word of Mason's success got out, patients with the same disease flocked to his office seeking the same treatment. Mason was not able to replicate his success however, because he fell victim to the current of disbelief:

> After that first patient, Mason was fully aware that he was treating what everyone in the medical establishment knew to be a congenital, "incurable" disease. Mason tried to pretend that

> he was upbeat about the prognosis, but he told the Discovery Health Channel, "I was acting."
>
> How could Mason's belief about that treatment affect its outcome..? The logical corollary is that the mind (energy) and body (matter) are similarly bound (as with entanglement), though Western medicine has tried valiantly to separate them for hundreds of years.

In this example, Lipton illustrates how belief is not only important in the mind of the patient, but also in that of the practitioner. Mason had doubted himself, and though he "acted" as though he still believed in the power of the mind to heal, the sinister reputation of the disease caused him to doubt the power of the mind to heal. Consciousness and the body—mind and matter—are intricately connected.

In his video, *New Biology*[14], Lipton asserts that as a species, we control our environment and the health of the planet, as well. He compares how mass thinking creates the rise and fall of societies in much the same way one's thinking creates the rise and fall of communities within the body (organs, tissues, etc.). People for eons have sensed this mind-body connection but are just beginning to notice the power of collective thought in terms of affecting the planet.

Our unified consciousness then, creates both the world we live in and the bodies we inhabit. Lipton says Charles Darwin's *survival of the fittest* theory is at best superficial, because it is *cooperation* and not competition that sustains our existence bodily and planetarily.

Ironically, a statement made by Darwin may give his proponents the courage to accept this change in thinking and the emerging science behind it:

> "It is not the strongest or most intelligent of species that survives, but the one most responsive to change."

Only when our beliefs change can we begin to control that which we normally think of as beyond our control. Healers, for example,

---

[14] *New Biology* (Lipton, Bruce. Spirit 200 Publishing, 2000. Video stream from HayHouse.com)

demonstrate the power we all hold to heal ourselves, but it is their belief that enables the healing and fortifies that of the one being healed.

This is not to say that belief comes easy. While we may say we believe in our innate powers to heal, we are deeply conditioned by society not to believe it is so. Even those with exceptionally strong belief may fail in controlling their health. Why is this? It comes back of course, to our oneness.

As we are all of one consciousness, even the most avid believer is held down by the overriding collective belief. That's why it's important we nurture each other not only physically, but spiritually. As one-by-one we change our thinking, we work toward lifting the whole of humanity to a higher level of being.

This goes beyond the power to heal. As Jesus pointed out, we are all endowed with the same powers he demonstrated, it's just that we have not yet reached our full potential (our full capacity to believe). When his disciples questioned why they could not cast out demons that caused an afflicted boy's epileptic seizures, Jesus responded:

> "Because of your unbelief; for assuredly, I say to you, if you have faith as a mustard seed, you will say to this mountain, 'Move from here to there,' and it will move; and nothing will be impossible for you. (Matthew 17:20).

As we collectively begin to remember our true identity and our faith increases—whether by means of personal spiritual experience, scientific discovery, or other means of awakening—our divine gifts manifest.

Herbert Bruce Puryear in his book, *Why Jesus Taught Reincarnation*[15], notes Biblical passages regarding our God-given gifts of the spirit:

> Now there are diversities of gifts, but the same Spirit. And there are differences of administrations, but the same Lord. And there are diversities of operations, but it is the same God which worketh all in all. But the manifestation of the spirit is given to every man to profit whithal. (I Cor. 12:4-7)

---

[15] Puryear, Herbert Bruce. *Why Jesus Taught Reincarnation. A Better News Gospel.* Scottsdale, AZ: New Paradigm Press, 1992.

Puryear specifically names these gifts as telepathy, clairvoyance, precognition, psychokinesis, healing, out-of-body experiences, communication with the dead, auras, meditation, astrology, reincarnation and past-life recall. While the labels may make some squeamish, as these abilities are most often associated with charlatans, it is not wise to throw the baby out with the bathwater.

More than ever, people of all backgrounds are awakening to their gifts and even those in traditionally "skeptical" fields of work, are no longer afraid to share their experiences. The elements of my own STEs encompass several of these gifts, which you will recognize as my story progresses. Dr. Dossey experienced profound instances of pre-cognition. Dr. Alexander most definitely had an out-of-body experience and communication with the dead (spoiler alert: his guide in Heaven turned out to be his deceased biological sister). Dr. Parti has become a consciousness-based healer. The list of credible professionals is numerous and continues to grow.

While we may seem to have individual gifts, I believe each of us has all these divine powers. At this point in our spiritual development however, we are only able to access those which are dominant within us as individuals ("differences of administration" as it is called in I Corinthians 12:4-7). As our belief grows, so do our abilities. It is no more mysterious than understanding that our gifts come from our ability to access the universal consciousness, the one mind.

Remembering who we are is part of our spiritual growth. Humanity's identity crisis however, cannot be blamed solely on the Church. The Church has been merely a roadblock in our spiritual evolution (this is not to say it hasn't done its part toward bettering us in many ways). Our forgetfulness, as I was about to find out, is intentional and our suffering designed to teach us unconditional love. As children of God, you might say we've reached young adulthood, we've passed our rebellious teenage years and can look upon our difficulties, challenges and suffering anew. All we've been through up to this point has kept us on the path to maturity, to reaching our full, divine potential.

Another Mystical Interlude

Ironically (or not), as Eric and I sat together over sushi one afternoon, I pondered the idea of using a quote at the beginning of this book. I whined about not finding anything unique enough to fit both my background (particularly as a prior proponent of evolution) and my relatively new worldview. Charles Darwin must have been listening because I popped open the cap on my bottle of Honest Iced Tea and found the perfect quote, which I ended up using in the previous paragraph as well. As I've proceeded through my spiritual journey, I've come to realize there are no coincidences!

CHAPTER EIGHT

A PAST LIFE REVEALED

A week after my vision of Jesus, Eric prepared to jet off to Europe on his first trip since my experiences began. He smoothed out a white button-down shirt on the bed, crossed one sleeve over the other, and then made a series of quick folds that magically transformed it into a neat rectangle as perfect as the day it had been packaged. He pressed it down on a stack of identical shirts, logos face-up like proud military badges. I've always marveled at his laundry aptitude.

"Can I help?" I asked, knowing full well anything I folded would end up being a do-over. It was part of the somber pre-business-trip routine. I thought about how he learned to fold with such precision during his time as a tank commander in the Royal Netherlands Infantry. More so, I silently thanked his mother for her unbiased teaching of domestic skills.

"I'm going to have to miss you again for three weeks," I whined through the pillow I clutched to my chest.

"Nineteen days," he corrected, giving me a quick, comforting kiss while un-balling his socks from the drawer to fold them properly for packing. I'd previously been the one on laundry duty.

While it was true I would miss him, this time was different. My mind was racing ahead to unspecified reading and a full-throttle investigation into my spiritual experiences. I wasn't yet sure what Eric thought of my strange encounters. I was wading in new waters and didn't want to inadvertently sink our relationship. I'd heard plenty of stories where one spouse "found God" and the other couldn't deal with the competition.

Several years after my STEs, a movie called *The Case for Christ* was released. It chronicles the true story of award-winning *Chicago Tribune* reporter Lee Strobel, who clashed with his wife Leslie over her new-found faith derived from an occurrence of Divine intervention that saved their young daughter's life. The couple had entered into marriage as avowed atheists, and Lee viewed them as smarter than average for not believing in religious or spiritual nonsense. As Leslie's faith grows, Lee secretly conducts a reporter-style investigation to disprove Jesus's divinity. In the end, Lee is overwhelmed by the evidence supporting Jesus's claim to be the Son of God, and he comes to faith as well.

Watching the movie I sympathized with Leslie, recalling my own hesitation to share my quickly evolving spirituality with Eric. Both he and I had a distaste for religion, and though we believed in the possibility of God, that's where our belief stopped. In the thirteen years we'd been together, I could not recall one discussion we'd had about religion or spirituality. It was simply not part of our lives. After my first two experiences, we both outwardly attributed my STEs to explainable causes. The angels were probably just Jehovah's Witnesses canvassing the neighborhood, and my vision of Christ just a dream.

I played along because, for the most part, I still believed there could be nothing more—and I didn't want Eric to think I'd gone AWOL! He expressed a lackadaisical irreverence whenever I approached the subject, saying his thinking didn't go that far (philosophically), so I mostly refrained from talking about it. Inside, I was burning to pursue the mystery, and like Leslie Strobel, I knew in the depths of my soul God had come calling.

We arrived at Newark Airport the customary two hours before Eric's scheduled flight. I hopped out of the passenger seat and circled around to the trunk, holding out my hand to receive the keys. Our old gray Volkswagen Routan proved handy in hauling the extra baggage of heavy-duty machinery and tradeshow paraphernalia Eric would have to tote around Europe. The van had seen its glory days, carrying our family on vacations from Ohio to various destinations in the U.S., including Florida—all the way down to Miami and back more than once—and a roundtrip to Colorado, during which I deemed it mandatory my children become familiar with the musical stylings of John Denver.

I rubbed my thumb back and forth over a rusted paint blister as I waited for Eric to unload his baggage. I felt a wave of sympathy for him as he hoisted a bulging backpack onto his shoulders, then yanked simultaneously on the telescoping handles of the two precariously stacked towers of luggage. He leaned forward and I threw my arms around his neck for a semi-passionate goodbye kiss, then I was on my own again.

In ninety minutes, Newark Airport was far behind me and the Barnes and Noble Bookstore just ahead. On a mission, I exited the highway and soon veered into the parking lot. Foregoing my usual routine of examining sale books in the vestibule, I headed straight for the information desk.

"Where can I find books on religion?" I asked, not having browsed that section before.

The woman mumbled something and pointed to the back, left area of the store. I didn't ask questions but followed my intended path.

I scanned the general subject matter on each shelf. The first two aisles held titles too typical to garner my interest, primarily Bible study or daily affirmations. I rounded another corner into the realm of spirituality, baulking at the metal plate with the inscription "New Age Mysticism" etched onto it. I was vaguely aware of the negative connotation. To me it had a 1970s hippie vibe. Nonetheless, I had never cared much for labels.

There was no shortage of books with "angels" in the title. I must have thumbed through every one of them before settling on two: *Proof of Angels*[16], and *Angels in My Hair*[17]. The subtitle of another drew my hand like a magnet, and I placed it on top of the pile without leafing through it: *Real Messages from Heaven…and Other True Stories of Miracles, Divine Intervention & Supernatural Occurrences*[18]. It described my situation perfectly.

I circled back to the religion area after scouring the titles in the hippie section, which had offered nothing up on Jesus. There were several Bibles, but I had one of those at home. My stepmother had given it to me for Christmas years earlier, and I had tucked it away in the bottom drawer of my nightstand, never to be seen again. Besides, I

---

[16] Ptolemy, Tompkins and Beddoes, Tyler. *Proof of Angels*. New York: Howard Books, 2016.

[17] Byrne, Lorna. *Angels in My Hair*. New York: Penguin Random House, 2008.

[18] Aldridge, Faye. *Real Messages from Heaven, and Other True Stories of Miracles, Divine Intervention & Supernatural Occurrences*. Shippensburg, PA: Destiny Image Publishers, 2011

wasn't keen on reading it. I was still agnostic and had an aversion to its tainted history and outdated language.

I was looking for something more like *When Jesus Appears and You Ask a Stupid Question*, or *What to Expect When You're Not Expecting Jesus*, or *Chicken Soup for Souls Who've Seen Jesus and Wonder What Comes Next*. We need those kinds of titles. Unfortunately, nothing came close. I settled on one that almost hit the mark, *Experiencing God*[19], by Henry and Richard Blackaby. The jacket's description acknowledged visions. I heaped the book onto my stack and did a quick tally of the cost. I nearly slid *God* back onto the shelf before making a beeline for the register.

The next weeks proved to be eye-opening for more reasons than one. A couple months earlier I wouldn't have bothered reading beyond the first few pages of any of these books. Now I approached everything from a new, more open perspective. Good thing, too. I would need that reverence for what would happen next.

One evening, snuggled on the couch under my favorite brown velvet blanket, reading material and iPad at hand, I came across the subject of reincarnation. This was not the first time I encountered it in my new curriculum, but normally I skipped over it and anything else I felt too new-agey to warrant my time. Contemplating the reality of God, Jesus and angels was enough on my plate. However, the last few paragraphs about reincarnation wrapped-up the article I was reading, and so I decided to finish it before going to bed.

Minutes later my iPad fell forward onto my chest and woke me up. I'd barely made it through the next few sentences, let alone the last few paragraphs. I rose off the couch and tidied up for the night, folding my blanket, tossing the pillows back in place, and lowering the blinds. As I did, I thought fleetingly about reincarnation in light of the messages I'd received.

If we are one with God then we must be eternal beings, I reasoned. *Reincarnation might make sense if we truly never die. What else would we do with so much time on our hands?*

As these simple thoughts crossed my mind, I picked up my books

19   Blackaby, Henry and Richard, and King, Claude. *Experiencing God. Knowing and Doing the Will of God*. Nashville, TN: B&H Publishing Group, 2008.

and iPad, slipped my pinky finger under the rubber loop on my water bottle and headed for the bedroom. As usual I stopped in the kitchen for a refill, unscrewing the lid and lodging my big 32-ounce Rubbermaid tumbler under the refrigerator's water dispenser.

As I waited, I picked up a pen and Post-it pad laying on the counter and lazily wrote the name "Rachel" in cursive, thinking, *I've always liked the name Rachel. Maybe because I was a 'Rachel' before.*

I dropped the pen and dislodged the water bottle before it could overflow, then screwed the lid on again. Chiding myself, I tore off the post-it with 'Rachel' scrawled on it, crumpled it and tossed it into the trash.

"Now that's just ridiculous," I mumbled.

I always sleep on the side of the bed closest to the window, even when Eric's gone and I could stretch out to my heart's content. I like being as close to nature as possible, and from my side of the bed, I can stare out at the night sky and contemplate life and, yes, send up a prayer for good measure. Lately my prayers had become a little more heartfelt considering I'd seen Jesus—but they were still pretty basic and I wasn't yet convinced of what was real.

I offered up the usual, giving thanks for my family and all that I had, and asked for my family's safety and continued good health. Just as I dozed off, no longer able to fend off sleep, I casually tacked on an off-the-cuff request:

— *And, God, if reincarnation is real, have I ever lived before, and if so, who was I? Amen.*

I don't know how long I'd been asleep, only that I was in a deep, peaceful sleep when I was abruptly awakened. I did not open my eyes, but my consciousness became fully aware. My attention was directed once again forward and slightly to the left (as it had been when Jesus visited). Then, the strangest thing that ever occurred in my life happened.

A letter came forward out of a white, misty background—a capital "A." Then another letter—a lowercase "b"—slowly followed, ending in position next to the now-faint "A." Letters continued to come forward and fade in this manner. Next was a lowercase "s." I became aware that a word—a name!—was being spelled-out. I sounded it out in my mind as each new letter appeared. Whoever was giving me the name was making sure I had it right.

I enunciated "Abs —" Another "a" came forward and I started over, "Absa —" Next came an "l," then an "o." Finally the last letter moved into place, "m."

A-b-s-a-l-o-m.

As I finished pronouncing it, the scenario repeated, but this time a little quicker. I said the name more confidently, pronouncing it now per syllable as the letters lined-up to form the name a second time:

Ab-sa-lom.

The scenario repeated a third time at yet a quicker pace. It flowed fluently in my awareness now and I pronounced it perfectly:

Absalom.

As the "m" moved into place and I stated the name, I noticed something that had not been there before. The entire name was coming from a paragraph located at the top right-hand corner page of a book. Behind each letter appeared projector-like rays of light, streaming the name "Absalom" forward from where it was printed. This was not any ordinary book, though. It was the Bible. The distinct look of thin, nearly translucent pages, small print, numbered and bolded paragraphs, chapter and verse headings made it unmistakable—even though the only text I could make out was "Absalom."

With that, my eyes flew open and I bolted upright in bed. I realized without a doubt that God had just provided me with a direct answer to a direct question I had asked him immediately before falling asleep. I was stunned.

Needing to reconnect to reality, I said aloud just to hear my own voice, "God just gave me an answer," then I looked around the room and whispered, "Thank you." I felt God was *right there beside me* as the first rays of dawn trickled through my bedroom window.

Heart pounding, I threw the quilt off me, jumped out of bed and crouched on the floor next to my nightstand. I pulled open the bottom drawer and dug through an agglomeration of junk: nearly empty lotion bottles, old cell phone cases, and magazines I would never read again. I tossed it all aside in a frenzy looking for the Bible my stepmother had given me. I thrust my hand under a pile of old receipts and greeting cards until my fingers graced the textured leatherette cover. Yanking it out of its hiding place, I peeled off a remnant of old tape and wrapping paper from the back cover and hopped back onto the bed, hunching over the Bible in eager anticipation of finding Absalom's story.

To my amazement, I opened the Bible to the *exact page* that displayed Absalom's name as I had seen it! I'd simply parted the Book with my thumbs and there it was—no flipping or turning of pages whatsoever. I was stunned for the second time that morning. *Whoa* was the only thing I could utter, still lost in the surreal moment.

There in the King James Version of the Holy Bible my stepmother had given me, in the first paragraph of the top, right-hand column of page 447, 2 Samuel 16:1, was the precise location Absalom's name had been projected off the page. I believe God's hand was on that very Bible that very morning in my very bedroom. In my excitement I could barely focus on what I was reading, but I quickly noticed I had been dropped into the middle of the story. I backed up a few pages and began reading from 2 Samuel 13:1.

> And it came to pass after this, that Absalom the son of David had a fair sister, whose name was Tamar; and Amnon the son of David loved her.

And this is where the trouble begins.

CHAPTER NINE

MAYHEM IN DAVID'S KINGDOM

T he trouble of which I speak is twofold: trouble in David's kingdom no thanks to Absalom; and trouble for me as I tried desperately to grasp how I could have been such a person. He was a murderer and a traitor. Parents throughout the ages dramatized his story as a warning against disloyalty by encouraging their children to throw rocks at his monument—one he had commissioned to honor himself.

Absalom was the much beloved third son of King David. As I read through 2 Samuel for the first time sitting there on the bed, I realized that David was *the* David of Biblical lore, of whom I'd heard, but knew nothing about. He was the second king of Israel, hand-picked by God to replace the first king, Saul, who'd stopped obeying God. More importantly, it was from David's lineage that God promised the King of Kings, Jesus, would spring. He was the same David of *David and Goliath* fame. The self-same David-as-musician said to have composed the Psalms. *This* David was my father in a past life. As if coming to grips with being Absalom was not enough!

I'd known none of this, nor had I ever heard of Absalom, before God answered my question. What I did sense, is that Absalom was the key to unlocking the mystery of reincarnation and that of my very soul. I took a deep breath and a giant step backwards into my past life.

I cannot begin to convey how crazy I know this sounds. Nor can I stress enough my internal battle to believe that not only had God revealed this to me, but he was imparting knowledge with major implications that would change my way of thinking entirely. So preoccupied was I with trying to understand God's messages for my own life, that I barely gave thought to what this meant for the world, for all of humanity.

Out of approximately nineteen legitimate sons from multiple wives and many more children from a multitude of concubines, Absalom was the favorite son of David. Both Absalom and his sister Tamar were of full royal lineage, their mother Macaah being the daughter of the king of Geshur, a neighboring province. Absalom had been educated and versed in soldiering skills, something David would have admired having been a celebrated soldier himself. We learn throughout the course of Absalom's story that he was charismatic, and he and his sister were admired for their beauty, and Absalom, especially, for his long, beautiful hair:

> But in all Israel there was none to be so much praised as Absalom for his beauty: from the sole of his foot even to the crown of his head there was no blemish in him.
>
> And when he polled his head, (for it was at every year's end that he polled it: because the hair was heavy on him, therefore he polled it) he weighed the hair of his head at two hundred shekels after the king's weight. (2 Sam.14:25-26)

While Absalom's physical appearance served him well, his sister's beauty made her the unhealthy object of desire of her older half-brother Amnon, who was "So vexed, that he fell sick for his sister Tamar; for she was a virgin; and Amnon thought it hard for him to do anything to her." (2 Sam. 13:2)

It was this perverse passion that drove Amnon to commit a grave sin, spurred on by his unscrupulous half-brother Jonadab. The scenes play out like a modern docudrama:

One day with nothing better to do, Jonadab is hanging out at Amnon's house in the wealthy section of town. He goads Amnon for his recent refusals to join the nightly partying, and especially for not taking advantage of his status as the king's son to lure women to his bedroom. Something is wrong, and Jonadab wants to know why.

Amnon finally laments, "I love Tamar, my brother Absalom's sister." (2 Sam. 13:4)

I picture Amnon sitting, head in hands, running his fingers through his hair as he declares what he knows is taboo. Although inter-familial marriage was common at the time, Amnon's "love" was merely lust, and Tamar being a virgin both excited and discouraged him because she was off limits in the way he desired. Had Tamar been just another girl in town, what happens next would not have changed the entire history of David's family.

Jonadab responds to Amnon by concocting a plan. He tells him to pretend he's ill and to ask his father to send Tamar to take care of him. Then he can do as he pleases with her.

In the next verse, Amnon makes himself sick. We're not told how; perhaps he holds the proverbial thermometer next to his bed lamp to feign fever. He calls his father to his house and whines, "I feel really sick today. Sorry I can't tend to my royal duties. Maybe if I could eat something… But I think the only thing I can stomach is those biscuits my sister Tamar makes. Maybe she could come over and make them for me? Maybe she could keep me company, too. I feel so awful." (Quotes are mine. I am taking creative liberties here.)

David complies, and when he leaves, Amnon suddenly feels better. He is mesmerized by Tamar and hovers over her as she sifts the flour and kneads the dough. Once baked, she sets the biscuits before her brother but he refuses to eat, suddenly ordering all his buddies to leave the house. The sly Jonadab must have delighted at seeing his plan in action. I imagine him snickering under his breath as Amnon prowls around Tamar like a wolf.

Amnon retires to his chamber, calling to his sister to feed him there. She carries in the biscuits, but as she raises the first bite to Amnon's lips he ensnares her and pulls her into bed. A struggle ensues as she cries out:

> And she answered him, "Nay, my brother, do not force me; for no such thing ought to be done in Israel: do not thou this folly.
>
> And I, whither shall I cause my shame to go? And as for thee, thou shalt be as one of the fools in Israel. Now therefore, I pray thee, speak unto the king; for he will not withhold me from thee." (2 Sam. 13:12-13)

Her plea falls on deaf ears, and Amnon rapes her. Immediately afterward, he has her thrown out of his house and into the street, her garments torn and tears streaming down her face.

> Then Amnon hated her exceedingly; so that the hatred
> wherewith he hated her was greater than the love wherewith
> he had loved her. (2 Sam. 13:15)

Had he cared for her, their father would have given his blessing to the relationship and they could have married. Instead, Tamar is now tainted and unworthy of marriage.

As she makes her way home, she runs into Absalom, who knows immediately what has happened. Tamar confirms his suspicion. Absalom comforts her, and we're told she lives out the remainder of her life in his house.

As soon as Absalom hears of Amnon's foul deed, he rushes to tell his father, expecting Amnon to be punished. We're told that while David is wroth over the situation, he does nothing. Perhaps it was his own guilt over falling for Amnon's scheme that prevented him from taking action. Based on Absalom's immediate hunch that Tamar had been raped by Amnon, it appears the family was already on high alert regarding his obsession.

Two years pass as Absalom waits patiently for his father to mete out justice. During that time, Absalom refuses to speak to his brother and his hatred grows until he can wait no longer and decides to take justice into his own hands:

> And Absalom came to the king, and said, "Behold now, thy
> servant hath sheepshearers; let the king, I beseech thee, and
> his servants go with thy servant."
>
> And the king said to Absalom, "Nay, my son, let us not all now
> go, lest we be chargeable unto thee." And he pressed him:
> howbeit he would not go, but blessed him.
>
> Then said Absalom, "If not, I pray thee, let my brother Amnon
> go with us. And the king said unto him, "Why should he go with
> thee?" (2 Sam. 13:24-26)

Absalom uses a successful sheep shearing season as an excuse to throw a party, which we're told will take place in Baalhazor beside Ephraim, a wooded area some distance from the palace. David responds that not all can go because no one would be in Jerusalem to watch over the city. He volunteers to stay behind but grants permission for Absalom's brothers to go and enjoy the party. Absalom suggests that Amnon go in his father's place, having predicted the king would not attend. David is surprised because Absalom had not forgiven his brother nor talked to him in two years. Absalom gives him the impression he wants to mend the relationship. David agrees to the request, once again deceived by a son.

Here, Absalom's revenge is laid bare:

> Now Absalom had commanded his servants, saying, "Mark ye now when Amnon's heart is merry with wine, and when I say unto you, 'Smite Amnon,' then kill him, fear not: have not I commanded you? Be courageous, and be valiant." (2 Sam. 13:28)

Amnon is struck down and the brothers scatter in fear. News is relayed to the king, but the message is distorted on the way from Ephraim to Jerusalem. The errant information was that *all* of David's sons had been killed by Absalom. David falls to the floor, tearing at his clothes in despair. Jonadab rushes to the king's side, comforting him with the speculation that only Amnon was killed, for he suspected Absalom harbored revenge from the day Tamar was raped. His assessment is confirmed when David's sons are spotted riding mules over the hillside on their way to a tearful reunion with their father.

David is overjoyed his sons are alive, but strangely does not express grief over Amnon's death. Instead, he laments the absence of Absalom, who fled to Geshur after his crime.

> And the soul of king David longed to go forth unto Absalom: for he was comforted (relieved) concerning Amnon, seeing he was dead. (2 Sam.14:39)

Three years pass, and David becomes increasingly sad over Absalom's absence. Another son intervenes to end his father's heartache, entreating a widowed village woman to present a false case to the king as part of a plan to reunite Absalom and David.

The widow tells David her two sons were working in the field when they began to argue. The fight escalated, and without their father to stop them, one killed the other. She says her family demands justice, calling for the first son to be executed for his crime. She begs the king to spare her remaining son. If he is killed, she argues, she will not have a son to carry on her husband's name, and there will be nobody to work the fields or take care of her.

David, reminded of the calamities in his own family, tells her to go home and he will think over his decision. Knowing the king has his already-damaged reputation to consider, the woman adds that he shouldn't pay attention to those who claim he's weak on justice, nor be persuaded against his own discernment. Her plea strikes a chord, and in a show of authority, David declares the living son should not be touched. Thanking him, the woman launches into a discourse about how he has done the right thing in the eyes of God—yet she wonders why he has let others' opinions keep him separated from his own son.

David suddenly recognizes the ruse, but understands Joab's intentions were good. He orders Absalom home again. However, he is still beholden to the court of public opinion. Not wanting to look weaker than he does already regarding matters of justice—especially after failing to punish Amnon—he decrees that Absalom can come home again but must live in his own house and never look upon the king's face again.

For two years Absalom abides by this rule, but eventually his patience wears thin again and he sends Joab with a message to his father:

> "Wherefore am I come from Geshur? It had been good for me to have been there still: now therefore let me see the king's face: and if there be any iniquity in me, let him kill me."

> So Joab came to the king, and told him; and when he had called for Absalom, he came to the king, and bowed himself on his face to the ground before the king: and the king kissed Absalom. (2 Sam. 15:32-33)

It didn't take much for Absalom to convince his father that two years of punishment was enough. All was good in the kingdom for a while, but Absalom could not forget his father's dispassionate neglect of justice. He blamed David for not punishing Amnon in the first place, which forced him to execute justice himself. That *he* was punished in a string of events that started with a crime perpetuated by Amnon, infuriated Absalom and he made sure everyone knew it.

In time, Absalom made a habit of standing at the city gates pre-judging cases brought to the king by the people. With his good looks and charming personality, Absalom attracted a following. He greeted travelers and listened with apparent great concern to their complaints, but warned them not to expect justice from his father. If he were king, he told them, things would be different.

> Absalom said moreover, "Oh that I were made judge in the land, that every man which hath any suit or cause might come unto me, and I would do him justice!"
>
> And it was so, that when any man came right to him to do him obeisance, he put forth his hand, and took him, and kissed him.
>
> And on this manner did Absalom to all Israel that came to the king for judgement: so Absalom stole the hearts of the men of Israel. (2 Sam. 15:4-6)

For forty years Absalom stood on his soapbox allowing his bitterness to consume him. Soon he devised another plan. This time he would kill his father and rule the kingdom. He was convinced he could do a better job, and by this time he had many supporters. Excusing himself to take care of unfinished business in Geshur, Absalom set up camp and launched his revolt. Many of David's closest subjects joined Absalom, including his father's most trusted advisor, Ahithophel.

When word of the revolt reached King David, he ordered all of his administration, soldiers, and family to flee with him. Six hundred made their way toward the wilderness carrying the Ark of the Covenant with them. In contrast to Absalom's rejection of his father's authority, David is seen as ready to accept God's will, no matter the outcome.

> And the king said unto Zadok, "Carry back the Ark of God into the city: if I shall find favour in the eyes of the Lord, he will bring me again, and shew me both it, and his habitation:

But if he thus say, 'I have no delight in thee'; behold, here am I, let him do to me as seemeth good unto him (according to his will)." (2 Sam. 14:25-26)

David instructs Zadok and his sons to remain in Jerusalem where they would be safe due to Zadok's status as a seer. He dispatches another advisor, Hushai, to return with them and pose as a supporter of Absalom. The strategy is for Hushai to become another counselor to Absalom, relaying the enemy's plans to Zadok, whose sons would sneak out of the city and relay them to David.

The ruse works and Absalom rejects Ahithophel's plan in favor of Hushai's. Ahithophel had proposed an immediate pursuit, saying David and his troops would be weak and tired from hurriedly fleeing the palace. Ahithophel suggests killing David only, and not his soldiers, to avoid a subsequent war, offering to kill David himself and encouraging Absalom to stay behind at the palace and enjoy his father's concubines. At this point, we learn Ahithophel has his own reasons for wanting to kill David and he counts on Absalom's sense of superiority and entitlement to enact his self-serving vengeance.

Hushai too, plays on Absalom's sense of superiority. He recommends Absalom begin acting as king, quickly establishing his rule so all tribes of Israel will see his greatness and rally behind him. Hushai counters Ahithophel's plan, saying rather than think David and his troops are weak, they are more like a mother bear set to defend her cubs. He reminds Absalom of his father's prowess as a warrior and that David has the strongest men in Israel with him. David himself would be slyly hiding away, he predicts. He advises Absalom that until he has further support, to hold off killing his father. Absalom agrees.

Meanwhile, the information makes its way to David via his spies. This gives him time to flee with his contingent over the Jordan River without fear of being caught in the open. He sets up camp in Gilead. Ironically, David's tendency toward forgiveness—often seen as weakness—serves him well, as formerly annexed enemies bring David a wealth of provisions to aid his defense.

Soon Absalom and his troops arrive in Gilead and a pivotal battle ensues. David gains control and issues the command that *his beloved son Absalom not be harmed.*

> And the king commanded Joab and Abishai and Ittai, saying, "Deal gently for my sake with the young man, even with Absalom." And all the people heard when the king gave all the captains charge concerning Absalom. (2 Sam. 18:5)

A battle ensues in Ephraim where, we are told, the forest is so dense it devours more people that day than the sword. In all, twenty thousand men die, and Absalom meets his fate at the hands of Joab.

> And Absalom met the servants of David, And Absalom rode upon a mule, and the mule went under the thick boughs of a great oak, and his head caught hold of the oak, and he was taken up (suspended) between the Heaven and the Earth; and the mule that was under him went away.
>
> And a certain man saw it, and told Joab, and said, "Behold, I saw Absalom hanged in an oak."
>
> And Joab said unto the man that told him, "And, behold, thou sawest him and why didst thou not smite him there to the ground? And I would have given thee ten shekels of silver, and a girdle."
>
> And the man said unto Joab, "Though I should receive a thousand shekels of silver in mine hand, yet would I not put forth mine hand against the king's son: for in our hearing the king charged thee and Abishai and Ittai, saying, 'Beware that none touch the young man Absalom.'" (2 Sam. 18:9-12)

Ignoring David's command to spare Absalom, Joab runs to find him still hanging in the tree and thrusts three darts (daggers) into his heart. Joab's men further defile his body by continuing to strike and spear him. Joab has Absalom's body tossed into a nearby pit, eliminating the chance

David would find his son's body and see the disrespect and damage done to it. So fearful was he, that he would not even allow his son to announce Absalom's death to the king, but tell him only that Absalom's forces had been subdued. He puts the burden of announcing Absalom's death on a different soldier. Upon hearing the news, David breaks down, too distraught to ask questions.

> And the king was much moved, and went up to the chamber over the gate, and wept: and as he went, thus he said, "O my son Absalom, my son, my son Absalom! Would God I had died for thee, O Absalom, my son, my son!" (2 Samuel 18:33)

What should have been a victory celebration turns into deep mourning, and David cannot contain his grief as he looks out over the city. In 2 Samuel 19:4 he continues wailing, "O my son Absalom, O Absalom, my son, my son!"

David's grief is so intense he forgets about the battle fought and won for him. His soldiers feel unappreciated, and Joab warns David he is in danger of losing his army. David pulls himself together and begins the task of re-establishing his kingdom. This is the last we hear about Absalom.

In keeping with his character, David pardons all those who sided with his son, even appointing Absalom's defeated commander as the new head of his army. This greatly reflects the difference between father and son. Absalom could not forgive and was driven to vengeance. David, on the other hand, was forgiving and compassionate and strived toward reconciliation. This is a perfect example of why God, in Acts 13:22, calls David, "...a man after my own heart."

CHAPTER TEN

NOTHING ALIKE

I t's not that David was perfect or that Absalom did not have redeeming qualities. The trouble between them, after all, began when Absalom felt overwhelming compassion for his sister, while David ignored the hideous crime of Amnon. I've read Absalom's story countless times endeavoring to see his life and struggles from different perspectives. In the beginning however, I was appalled by him, and didn't understand how I could have *been* him. I'm an innately understanding, accepting, and forgiving person. While far from perfect, the choices I've made in my life reflect this.

David and Absalom's story is one of familial strife. Hardly any family members get through life without hurting each other, and it was no different in my childhood home. There were bigger incidents and there were smaller ones involving me and my siblings and me and my parents. I could argue and get mad like the rest, but for the most part—and I'm sure my family will agree—I was the quiet one, the one most likely to let things go, and the most likely to apologize whether right or wrong. I am in no way trying to say I was perfect or better, because we all have good and bad qualities. I am trying to establish however, that compassion and forgiveness have been my nature from the beginning.

The same was—and still is—true of friendships. I'm more likely to have been hurt by a friend than to have been mad at one. Those who have hurt me, most likely do not even realize it because I probably did not address it. Not because I was afraid, but because I always tried to imagine why they'd done or said such a thing, whether on purpose or not. I usually ended up feeling sympathy for whomever may have hurt me.

Simple matters aside, there have been two major events in my life that would have brought the worst out in anyone. Like Absalom, I could have been spiteful, vengeful, held a grudge, and possibly pushed my actions to the extreme.

Divorce is never easy, and mine was no exception. Though amicable at first, things got messy later when it came to our daughter. I prefer to keep most details private, but there were several reasons I felt justified in my efforts to relocate with Bailey without interference from anyone. After three years of separation, I met Eric and was ready to move to Holland and begin a life with our combined family. I was completely shocked to be taken to court and dragged into a relocation and custody battle—one which cost me an inordinate amount of stress and financial difficulty. Ultimately I won full custody and relocation rights, but there were battle scars on both sides. The damage seemed irreparable.

I could have been vengeful and moved to Holland immediately after the court decision. It would have been easy to leave the mess behind. I was hurt and angry and didn't feel like a *winner*. Instead, I felt everyone's pain. I decided not to rush to Holland simply because I could. I viewed the legal outcome as providing me freedom to choose.

Eric continued to look for a job in the U.S., and was eventually offered a position that guaranteed him frequent travel back to Holland. It was the best solution for us, enabling Eric to see his children often, and my ex-husband and his family access to Bailey. In the ensuing years, Eric and Bailey's father and I developed a respectful friendship and a united front in raising her. I believe the outcome was fated, and everything worked out because I had remained compassionate toward all involved in the situation.

My mother's death tested me as well. She had discovered a secret about someone, and I warned her weeks before her passing to be careful, afraid she would suffer an "accident." It's not that I had a premonition, but it was a gut feeling based on what she'd uncovered. She was only fifty-six years old when she died. The official cause of death was congenital heart failure, but this can be induced, especially by someone with knowledge of drugs. That same someone in this case fought against an autopsy.

I spent many sleepless nights pondering what to do. I could fight for proof or I could let go of my suspicion. I knew no matter what I did or said, nothing would bring my mother back. I opted for the latter, but it wasn't easy. Even if my suspicion was incorrect, there were other behaviors enacted toward my mother that broke my heart. To move on, I had to forgive.

This is perhaps the hardest thing I ever had to do, but I did have help. The second night after my mother's death, she appeared to me. At that time, I had not had my STEs, and believed little in the possibility of after-death communication.

It happened much the same way Jesus appeared to me years later. My consciousness was awakened from a deep sleep, and I moved to the large picture window overlooking the courtyard of my apartment building. I looked down to see my mother sitting on a lounge chair. The moment I saw her, I immediately changed location and found myself standing in front of her. She had on a white robe and her hair was as she had worn it in her thirties. Rainbow-colored lights streamed from her face, and dark areas appeared where her eyes, nose, and mouth would be located. Most notably, I *felt* her presence. I knew with certainty it was her, but something was different.

"Mom! You're not angry anymore!" I exclaimed, not verbally, but in the same way I communicated years later with Jesus, telepathically.

She had been particularly bitter over unfolding events toward the end of her life. None of those emotions were present though, and she exuded happiness. I will never forget her response:

"That's not possible here," she said. I could feel joy emanating from her.

After her declaration, the vision dissipated and I was back in my body. I opened my eyes immediately and cried because it had been so real. Afterward, I had trouble feeling sad about her passing. I might have cried because I missed her, but I never again felt sad she had moved on.

Life of course is filled with challenges, and I've had plenty of opportunities to choose between forgiveness or not. I'm not perfect, but for the most part, I've chosen tolerance, acceptance, forgiveness and love. Absalom chose the opposite. His judgmental nature and unhinged compulsion for justice ruined the relationship he'd had with a loving father, and ultimately ended his life.

In the area of justice and punishment, I'm more like David. I believe our modern justice system has done nothing but harden criminals further. I am an advocate of rehabilitation over harsh punishment, and I do not believe in the death penalty. Had Absalom's revolt been successful, he no doubt would have served up countless death penalties, leading to fear-based obedience from his subjects. David conversely, was a tolerant and compassionate leader who earned loyalty through love.

In the beginning of my journey, I failed to find similarity between myself and Absalom (apart from the compassion he had for his sister), and I thought maybe God had made a mistake....

CHAPTER ELEVEN

CONFIRMATION I, THE TREE

I t was an early spring morning, no more than a week after I'd received the stunning revelation from God that I'd once lived as Absalom. Although still chilly, I'd already begun opening the main windows in the house in the mornings. Taking in the crisp air, the chirps of mother birds tending to their newborns, and the return of woodpeckers' distant, hollow jackhammering grounded me to the earth at a time when, more often than not, I felt caught up in dream.

It was a few days into Eric's business trip and I was feeling a bit lonely. The special "mommy-daughter days" Bailey and I shared whenever Eric traveled were a thing of the past. When she was younger, I sometimes called in sick and kept her home from school so we could spend an entire day together. We usually went to the zoo, a museum, or the movies to see the latest Disney flick, jaunting over to the mall food court to enjoy her favorite Chinese fast-food afterwards.

By the time she was in high school, those precious days had dwindled to sneaking away for a healthy shake at the local Smoothie King during her school lunch break. She was rarely home by the time I was able to quit my outside job, and we went to bed and woke up at different times. Eric and I felt like empty nesters before the hatchling had flown the coop. I thought of it as a prelude to college, bracing myself for the inevitable. No more would the tender-sweet smell of vanilla perfume linger near her bedroom, nor the plucking of guitar strings resonate from behind closed doors as she arranged and re-arranged lyrics to a brand new song. Sigh.

I cracked two eggs into a bowl, spooned the yolks out and let them slide down the drain, then seasoned the whites with salt and pepper before whipping them into a mundane version of an omelet. Some hot tea and a few slices of smoked salmon from the refrigerator rounded out my breakfast. I carried it precariously, along with my fork, napkin, and iPad, to the kitchen table positioning myself directly across the bay window and sliding glass doors leading to our deck. I tried to be quiet, not so much to avoid waking Bailey, who could sleep through a marching band on the weekends, but to avoid stirring Charlie, our twelve-year-old Cairn terrier whose ears never went up and who only left Bailey's side if he suspected someone was in the kitchen.

I generally read the newspaper with breakfast. Not the old-fashioned kind that leaves black ink on your fingertips, but the e-version. I took a bite of egg and connected to the internet, instantly bringing me to *msn. com*, my designated homepage and news feed. I tried to read a couple of articles, but couldn't focus and had to keep starting over.

My efforts were futile. All I could think about was the completely bizarre and seemingly supernatural things that were happening to me: the visit from angels telling me suffering would not last forever, the visit from Jesus and his message that we are all one, and now, being told I was Absalom and that reincarnation is real! This was not normal. As hard as I tried to sweep it all under a rug—to just ignore it and pretend it didn't happen—I couldn't. The experiences were too completely strange and powerful to deny. What did it all mean? Why was I receiving these communications? Were they truly *divine?* These questions, and the marvel of what was happening played on a continuous loop in my mind.

I stared out the glass sliders and sipped a second cup of hot tea, still bewildered over the latest encounter. I reflected on the name I was given, and couldn't quite remember it. It was in no way familiar. I don't remember ever having encountered it before that night. In fact it was so foreign to me, I had to return to the now-bookmarked section of 2 Samuel several times in the days that followed to familiarize myself with it.

"Ambulson —Almobob —Asbomloson." I struggled to get it right.

Oh yes, here it is, I said to myself as I turned a few pages to where I'd first seen the name on the upper right-hand corner of page 447: "Absalom." After a while the name rolled off my tongue.

I suppose I might have come across it at some point prior to the revelation that I had *been* Absalom, but I had no conscious recollection of it. Researching the name much later, I discovered it has been referenced throughout the ages in literature, art, music, and even video games to represent pride, resentment, control, jealousy, and rebellion. The

English poet John Dryden in 1681 penned "Absalom and Ahithophel," a satirical poem about Charles II overthrowing James, the Duke of York, to claim the English throne for himself. The novel *Absalom, Absalom!* is a prodigal son-type story written by William Faulkner. Tim Burton, a film director known for his oddly morbid cartoon features, gave the name "Absolem" (a slightly different spelling) to the caterpillar in his 2010 version of *Alice in Wonderland*. I had not seen the film, nor read any of the literature.

Music is rife with references to Absalom, from chorale music of the 1500s to twenty-first-century progressive metal music and everything in between. The band The Residents featured a song on their *Wormwood* album titled, "Hanging by His Hair," a dark piece featuring Middle Eastern-sounding woodwinds (you can find it on YouTube, if you dare). Ironically, in 2011, an insurgent group in northern Iraq released a song called, "Absalom," which is about King David's remorse over his son's death. One has to wonder whether someone in the group is a son of an Iraqi government official. Most notably, from the annals of religion, if one is said to have an "Absalom spirit," it means he embodies those less-than-desirable qualities exhibited by Absalom.

Even if I'd encountered "Absalom" in any context before my STEs, and the name was buried in my memory as an insignificant piece of information, I couldn't dismiss all the other astonishing details of this latest experience. I was awestruck by the fact God had heard me and answered me directly, not once, but now twice. Beyond that, it was he who had chosen to keep our conversation going by sending Jesus my way, despite my dismissal of his angels as a bizarre coincidence.

I walked to the sliding doors and rested my forehead on the cold glass, thinking back to my silly gesture before going to bed the night before my vision. I had amused myself by writing "Rachel" on a Post-it note. If I'd been dreaming, it would have made more sense for my brain to feed me back the name "Rachel", or at least something I would have recognized. I breathed on the glass and wrote "Absalom" with my finger, still digesting the completely foreign-sounding name. I walked absent mindedly into the living room, wrapped my brown throw around my shoulders, and sank into the couch just to think.

I marveled again at how real the dream had been. Just as when Jesus and my mother had appeared to me on separate occasions, I'd been suddenly awakened from a deep sleep. It took me a second to get my bearings, and then I instinctively knew to sound out the name as each letter was presented. Only when the vision was over, when my eyes flew open, did I realize I'd received another answer from God.

I dream a lot, as in almost every night, and remember most of them. Many are recurring. It's been that way since I was a kid, with the added oddities of sleepwalking and sleep talking. It seems my soul is quite active at night! I've learned on my spiritual journey that all dreams mean something, so it's important to pay attention to them. In all my life, however, I've *never, ever* dreamed of anything being spelled out to me. I believe God knew this vision had to be different from any dream I'd ever had before for me to realize it was his doing.

I poured another cup of hot water and dipped a new tea bag up and down as I stepped outside and sat on the deck landing, my feet on the first of three stairs leading to our brick patio. I wondered if it had been God or Jesus who'd answered me. I hadn't seen anyone this time, as I had when the angels came to my door, or when Jesus appeared to me. I laughed at the thought that perhaps I was being tag-teamed. Was I that difficult a case? I quickly remembered what Jesus had told me—that he and God are separate, but one. The question was a moot point.

I sat my empty cup aside and ventured a few more steps down to the patio, then onto the lawn. It felt good to be outside with my bare feet in the dewy grass, which was ankle-high and in need of mowing. I wrapped my blanket tighter around my shoulders and stared into the pale morning sky, pondering my vision, astonished at how I could have possibly opened the Bible to the *exact* page I had been shown. Had God been right there in my bedroom that morning? Had his hands been on mine, guiding my actions? The thought nearly moved me to tears. Charlie broke the silence, his barking loud and clear coming from Bailey's backyard-facing window. I trudged inside, set him free, and closed the bedroom door again.

Around midday Bailey flew past me and out the door to wherever teenagers go on Saturday afternoons. I grabbed a sweater and followed, hoping to chat a bit and find out what time she planned on being home, but she'd already backed out of the driveway in her hand-me-down P.T.

Cruiser. At least it was a convertible and a pretty French vanilla color to match her vanilla-scented perfume, although she didn't see it that way. It was Mom's old car—blah! I waved goodbye from the driveway and stood there long after she had turned the corner out of the neighborhood.

The sun felt especially comforting as I shuffled back up the driveway and milled around the garage, sweeping away a collection of dried bugs from the window sill with a broken snow brush that had been sticking upright in the trash can. I had no plans for the day, but I knew what needed to be done. I avoided looking at the lawn mower at all costs. As I searched for a less demanding chore, I was saved by the bell—sort of.

It was Eric calling from Germany. He'd worked a long day at a trade show and was heading out with clients to dinner before turning into bed early. We chatted about the usual stuff and I shared with him the new spiritual literature I was reading, careful not to make too much of it. He already knew about Absalom and my latest STE, which was difficult enough for both of us to swallow. I veered from the subject, telling him it was too nice a day to be inside. My mistake.

"I bet da grass is from here da Tokyo," he said.

"Well, it was already long when you left," I retorted. Pause. "I guess you want me to mow it?" I asked.

Of course he told me to have someone do it, but he was also aware that no service will come out for onesie mowings. Calling someone would mean signing a contract, and we are die-hard do-it-yourselfers. Well, I'm an indoor do-it-yourselfer, but I'd picked up several outdoor chores since taking on less marketing work and feeling guilty over my lighter workload and less stressful life. The snow blower and I had become good friends over the winter and now I was about to get reacquainted with the push mower.

"I'll call around and see if anyone can do it," I agreed, humoring him.

"Yeah, but don't let dem talk you into a contract or so," he said, effectively killing my grand scheme of having mowing service for the summer.

We said our syrupy good-byes and hung up. Defeated, I eyed the lawnmower then went inside and switched to an old pair of sneakers. Soon enough I was playing tug-of-war with the pull cord. Once I got past that, the massive slope on the side yard, and mowing around the in-ground trampoline and monster crevasse around it, which usually tried to swallow the mower whole, it would be smooth sailing.

I thought the rhythmic mowing and connection to solid ground might provide momentary escape from the heavy doses of reality I was being given. Such was not the case. I found myself reflecting again on Absalom—his character flaws, acts of violence and murder and betrayal—and recoiled at the thought that I could have been *him*. As I mowed I spoke directly to God, expressing my frustration. I could not understand how my soul, which seemed to me at the core to be genuinely caring and loving, could have committed such dastardly deeds.

And what about karma? I wondered in exasperation, suddenly realizing I might have to pay for Absalom's sins. I'd been a decent person in this life, and it didn't seem fair. Was my vision a warning of some kind of come-uppance?

If karma is real, I don't like the system, I fired at God.

I continued my line of questioning—which at times flowed into gibberish as I tried to make sense of reincarnation—for the entire two hours it took to mow our sloping yard.

Finally, reprieve—for both God and myself. I approached the final section of lawn to be mowed, an area bordering our back patio, which included a few fully grown trees and five or six young maples. These had never posed a problem and were tall enough that I had only to duck slightly to avoid branches. I purposely mowed this area last so I could reach through the kitchen sliders and grab the water bottle I had left for myself inside without tracking grass through the house. As usual, I would take a break on my reclining lounger and chug down my water before heading indoors to shower. I wrapped up my thus far one-sided conversation with God.

God, I deeply appreciate that you gave me an answer, I said (not aloud, but telepathically as I was getting used to), exasperated from both the physical and mental exertion.

But I need to know it wasn't a dream and if not, that you didn't make a mistake. Would you mind checking your records? I quipped.

I can't believe I was Absalom, I said. *I need a confirmation.*

I know—a ballsy thing to say to God. Maybe that's why I got such an immediate response.

At the precise moment I asked for a confirmation, an overhanging branch seemed to take hold of my ponytail—which I wear high toward the back of my head—giving it a very purposeful and forceful yank. I gasped, but *immediately* understood God's confirmation.

Similar to my other experiences, the exchange happened quickly. I'd barely formed the thoughts in my mind when the action occurred in immediate response. Incredibly, the entire scenario was accompanied by a sense of playfulness. I felt God's joy and we had a light-hearted chuckle together! I instantly understood God's confirmation that he had not made a mistake (go figure!), followed by the intentional and unaided release of my ponytail. I hadn't even had time to lift my hand to my head.

The significance of my hair getting caught in the tree is, of course, related to Absalom's death. The confirmation made perfect sense. Absalom's hair got tangled in a massive terebinth (oak) tree, leaving him hanging—caught between Heaven and Earth—when enemy soldiers caught up to him and killed him. That was end of Absalom's life—but apparently not the end of *his and my soul's* much greater journey.

CHAPTER TWELVE

CONFIRMATION II, IRELAND

Two months later I found myself looking out over the Cliffs of Moher, which stand at attention on the Irish coastline, beckoning sea birds to feather nests in their nooks and crannies well above the salty ocean spray. The cliffs—and all the western areas of the emerald isle—are magical. Even my stepchildren, who had winced at the thought of a rain-soaked vacation, were awestruck.

We clambered up the dirt path on our way to a paved trail that crested the cliffs, passing primitive looking barbed wire fencing on the way. Eric called ahead to our merry band of Irish rovers, comprised of our three children, plus one. It had been Bailey's turn to bring a friend along on our family vacation. We were happy to expose many of our kids' friends to new cultures and foreign lands, an opportunity they might never have had otherwise. While our family being split between two continents had its challenges, it had its benefits, too.

"Da fence is live," Eric shouted upwind after passing a sign that said so.

Bailey recoiled, having stuck her hand through the wires to pet a cow (as she later explained) just as Eric issued the warning. Her friend Katie laughed hysterically. With a painful tingle running up her arm and a slightly bruised ego, Bailey ran to catch up with the others, the three girls' long tresses whipping wildly in the Irish gale. I thought it ironic my Italian-Cuban-Cherokee raven-haired, olive-skinned progeny was one quarter Irish, with a name to match—*Bailey Ann Gallagher.* Jasper and Danique, with not a drop of Irish blood in 'em, could have passed for a typical lad and lassie with their fair skin and red-tinged hair.

Bailey was the only one of our teens to express immediate excitement when we told her our family vacation would be to Ireland. Her grandfather had emigrated as a young boy from Donegal with his parents, and she'd always wanted to visit his native country.

Jasper and Danique were less than thrilled. Born and raised in

Holland, a country technically below sea level with an average of 217 days of rain per year, sunshine was a top priority of any vacation. Unfortunately, Ireland has only three weather conditions: raining, about to rain, or just rained, as we learned from the funny weather quip plastered on everything from umbrellas to woolen socks in gift shops throughout the emerald isle.

"We'll take umbrellas and I'll buy everyone new rain jackets and waterproof sneakers before the trip," I'd promised. "Besides, it won't rain every day." I crossed my fingers and hoped for the best. Despite the daily drizzle, we did enjoy a sufficient amount of sunshine, and we were all captivated by Ireland.

The girls and I kissed the Blarney Stone, though the guys refused, too put off by cooties from hundreds of years of tourists' lip smacks. We attended a royal horse race where spectators were dressed in exquisite garb, including us girls, who donned cheap drugstore hair combs adorned with beads and plumage—a far cry from the mile-high fancy hats of the local beauties. We circled the Ring of Kerry, navigating the craggy landscape and touring a hidden perfumery that distilled the essence of nearby wildflowers. We marveled at Kylemore Abbey, purchased trinkets of Connemara marble as green as the emerald isle herself, and fought the raging sea on a fishing expedition, after which several of us had to ditch our new rain jackets due to vomit, grease, and fish guts. We also did our fair share of proving Ireland, new to the international culinary scene, was definitely a foodie paradise. The cuisine was world class!

We didn't know much about Ireland when we made the decision to go. In fact, we were not supposed to be going to Ireland in the first place. That's why my stepchildren were not initially thrilled with the idea—well, that and the rain.

Our vacations were always fabulous—not necessarily extravagant, but fabulous in that we thoroughly enjoyed being together. In the lean years, we often barely had enough money for a rental close to the beach or a rustic cabin in the woods. We made our own fun, taking walks, collecting and pressing wildflowers, playing board games, biking, and cooking together. Over the years, many friends and relatives offered their homes or rentals, enabling us to stay an entire week at the Lake

Erie Islands, Disney World, New York City, or the Cayman Islands. Between Europe, the U.S., and a few other dots on the map, we've covered a lot of ground.

So when Jasper and Danique seemed disappointed about Ireland, it was fleeting. They knew vacation, like life, is what you make of it. Our children have always been grateful for the opportunities they've had, including each and every one of our trips, big or small. When they became teens with after school jobs, they took it upon themselves to buy Eric and me a thank-you gift at the end of a trip, taking us to fancy restaurants surely beyond their financial means. What a joy to feel their appreciation!

As the kids matured, we included them in vacation planning. By 2013, the year we went to Ireland, they'd been giving their input for years. Usually, they agreed right away with what Eric and I proposed. In the previous two years, we'd taken a lot of city trips. We all loved history, science, and culture. Danique particularly liked art museums, as evidenced by her t-shirt purchased at the Andy Warhol Museum in Pittsburgh. None of us could keep a straight face as we ate at the Spaghetti Warehouse the evening after our museum visit. Danique sat nonchalantly at the head of the table wearing her plain black t-shirt with "Art Slut" written across the front. Our children definitely have a wicked sense of humor.

Having toured cities for a while, we unanimously decided a tropical beach would be a good change of pace. I was looking forward to sun, sand, and surf probably more than anyone. In addition to a chilly Ohio spring, I needed a respite from the intense immersion into spiritual matters. It had been only a few weeks prior to vacation planning when I received the confirmation that I had been Absalom. What I'd been experiencing was heavy duty stuff. Esteemed philosophers have driven themselves mad after all, trying to make sense of God, our purpose and mortality. The beach would be good for me.

I became an ace over the years at getting decent lodging at bargain-basement prices. Some places were better than others. Sometimes we'd have to stick a kid in a makeshift bed on a wide window sill during a one-night hotel room stay; but hey, if cutting corners was the way to have a great trip, we did it. I wrangled the best possible prices for everything from lodging to fancy dinners to swimming with dolphins, often swapping marketing services in exchange for discounts.

I was a week into scouring the internet for tropical vacation deals. My notebook looked like a football coach's playbook, arrows and lines crisscrossing in an effort to come up with the perfect destination, lodging, and activities that fit our budget. As Eric and I reclined on opposite ends of the couch one evening, I continued my quest via my iPad while Eric concentrated on a Sudoku puzzle, level: hard.

Cozumel, Miami, Puerto Rico, and Jamaica. I had four screens open for a bird's-eye view comparison when the same pop-up advertisement that had been doing its thing appeared again. I swiped it away, but this time Jamaica and Cozumel disappeared into the abyss, too.

"Uhg—this stupid thing!" I exclaimed.

"What is it?" Eric asked, setting aside his *Big Book of Sudoku* I'd gotten him the previous Christmas.

"It's a pop-up for *Ireland*. I can't get rid of it," I said.

Eric reached his hand out and I gladly turned over my iPad for him to remedy the situation permanently.

"Probably has something to do with cookies," I suggested, not really knowing what cookies were.

"Uh-huh," he said.

I maneuvered next to him to see what trick he'd use, suddenly remembering his best trick was to shut it down and start over.

I managed a high-pitched squeal before he could make a move. "Don't lose my other pages!"

The pop-up appeared again, and he clicked on it. With that, he changed our entire vacation plan.

"Wow. Dit you look at dis?" he asked.

"No. Why would I look at Ireland?" I shot back.

"Dis looks really cool." He was sucked in by images of towering castles and pints of Guinness dancing across the page.

"Uh—no." I reached for my iPad, but he jerked it away.

"I'm serious. Dis could be someting for us," he said.

I reminded him of the tropical beach, burying our toes in the warm sand, and crab legs in drawn butter. Succulent.

"Ireland has seafood. It's on da sea," he countered with his typical circular logic.

"Uh, no," I reiterated. "We're going to the tropics."

He didn't say anything but continued to take in the full glory of Ireland through the ad. I could see his wheels spinning.

"Wow. Dis is really cheap, too. Dit you see you da cost?" he asked, shoving the iPad under my nose and pointing to the promotion.

He drew me in. I was keeper of the financial vacation-planning keys. I quickly glanced at the details. It was a great deal.

After arguing his point some more, I suggested we propose it to the kids. There was one problem, though: the promotion ended that night. I quickly calculated the time. If it's 10 p.m. here, that means it's—11, 12, 1, 2, 3—3:00 o'clock in Holland—*a.m.* There was no way we could talk to Jasper and Danique before midnight, so we laid the entire decision on Bailey, calling her out of her rabbit hole to propose the change in plans.

"Uh— hell, yeah!" she answered, looking at us as if going to Ireland would even be a question.

I gave her the stink eye for cussing.

"Well, you know I've always wanted to go to Ireland. That would be sooooo amazing," she squealed. "I can't believe we're actually going."

"Hold on. We're not going yet. What about Jasper and Danique? What do you think they'd say? What about the tropical beach? What about the parasailing and the snorkeling and your tan?" I assailed her with questions.

"I think Jasper and Danique would looove it," she said wide-eyed. "We can go to the beach anytime."

"Dat's true," Eric chimed in. "Dare are always beach deals."

"Are you willing to speak for all three of you?" I asked Bailey. "Even if Jasper and Danique get mad at you for it?"

It was totally unfair to put her in such a position, but she had no qualms about taking the heat.

"Yes. If it means we're going to Ireland, then hel—uh, heck—yes!" She still couldn't believe it was even in debate.

"I guess we go to Ireland, den!" Eric proclaimed victoriously.

The sun, sand, and surf slipped below the pinkish-orange tropical horizon in my mind and out of my hands for good.

"Woohoo! I can't believe I'm going to Ireland!" Bailey shouted, dancing her way back to her rabbit hole.

For the first time ever, we booked a vacation without everyone having a say.

Two and a half months later the three of us, plus Bailey's friend, Katie, landed in Dublin. Jasper and Danique's flight landed less than an hour later, and we shuffled out to the rental car lot where our large-for-Europe compact car was waiting. It had two rows of back seats, which were necessary to accommodate six, but it was still a foreign compact—meaning we were cramped. Really cramped. On the drive from the airport to the resort, we crammed our luggage in wherever we could. We sat on it, put it on the floorboards with our legs pinned to our chests, and shoved it between the driver and passenger seats. On the nearly three-hour drive, we discovered there is nary a smooth road to be found in western Ireland. It was so bad that Bailey, the smallest of the group and relegated to the back seat for the entire vacation, donned her half-moon-shaped travel pillow as a hat to cushion the constant blows to her head. We had some good laughs at her expense.

By evening, we settled into the condo-style rental located on an old, rugged golf course. Far from resort status by tropical beach standards, it met our expectations and basic needs. Unfortunately, it was nearly a two-hour drive from most everything on our "must do" list. We had known this up front, but decided the weekly promotional rate was worth it. We hadn't anticipated the bumpy roads.

Tired, we headed to our rooms after briefly touring the grounds. It started to drizzle as we returned, then became a full-fledged downpour just as we snuggled into our beds. It had been a long day, and the condo was chilly. Eric fell asleep as soon as his head hit the pillow. I was mesmerized by the rain hitting the skylight directly overhead.

Absalom entered my thoughts as I stared up into the night sky. The vastness of space had me feeling vulnerable and doubt set-in again. I questioned the reality of the confirmation I'd been given. More than once I'd gone out to the area of grass beneath the maple trees in my back yard to reenact the moment. I adjusted my pony tail to make sure it was high enough, offering it up as I ducked slightly and followed my mowing path. I kept my arms at my sides instead of holding on to an imaginary mower, not wanting the neighbors to think I'd lost my mind. Nothing happened, except the rustling of leaves. I tried again, walking fully upright, wriggling my head almost forcing my hair to get tangled in the branches. Nothing.

While I could hardly deny to myself any longer that God was communicating with me, I began to convince myself that my hair had merely gotten caught in the tree. I ignored the lighthearted moment of joy I'd seemed to share with God. Surely that was all in my head.

As I puzzled over the mystery of reincarnation and Absalom, the rain pelted the skylight harder and I began to drift off. Before I was out for good though, I asked God for *one more* confirmation, something unmistakably having to do with Absalom.

We arose late the next morning, most of us suffering jet lag. By the time we had unpacked and showered, it was past noon. The sun was shining and Eric and Jasper walked to the neighboring building to pick up brochures at the reception desk and ask whether there was anything to do nearby. We didn't want to venture far and preferred to take it easy our first day. Turns out, there was a castle with a folk park only fifteen minutes away. It was the only thing touristy nearby. In fact, it was the only thing at all nearby. There was a reason we'd gotten such a good deal on accommodations. So the castle it was.

I'd never heard of Bunratty. Our itinerary had a couple of famous castles on it, but I didn't want to overdo it, so I hadn't considered more. I skimmed the two Ireland travel books I'd brought with me. There was nothing in the thick one, but the skinnier "Walks and Tours" guide had two small paragraphs referring to the structure as technically a medieval tower house. There was much more description about the recreated village and pecking hens than there was about the castle itself. The description played on the word "blarney" to draw in visitors more familiar with the famous Blarney Castle. I didn't expect much.

Once the girls finished primping, we piled into our backpack on wheels, as Eric called it, and headed down the road. I dozed off despite the jarring ride, but woke a few minutes later to the sound of gravel crushing beneath the tires as we pulled into the parking lot. The castle loomed in the distance, more impressive than I had anticipated.

We purchased our tickets at the booth outside the gate, and the cashier handed us a complimentary booklet. The castle, restored in 1854, was originally built in 1425 and contained artifacts from the fifteenth and sixteenth centuries, including furniture, art, cookware, washing vessels, and hunting weapons. Large regency-style gardens graced the property, the originals of which would have supplied fruits, vegetables and flowers for the house's inhabitants. Now they supplied the restaurants in the folk village, including one ironically called *Gallagher's*, Bailey's last name. As we strolled past flowered terraces on the way to the main entrance, a bizarre display of cannonball-sized eyeballs scattered throughout the landscape seemed to surreptitiously watch our every move. It gave me an eerie feeling, but things were about to get even more strange.

Attendance at the park was light and we sauntered through the grand archway, entering the cavernous Great Hall. The approximately thirty-five-foot-high ceiling was covered in dark wood planks with simple arched trusses running its length, the arms of each extending down over white stone walls flanked on both sides with folk carvings of angels. Three sets of enormous primitive deer antlers hung over the doorways at opposing ends of the hall, and a single banquet table sat elevated at one end. The rectangular space was lined with modern benches for visitors, interspersed with heavy, wooden period-pieces of furniture.

Across the Great Hall from the entrance door near where we stood, about twenty feet away, was a balding, grey-haired man in his early sixties, dressed conservatively in khakis and a button-down shirt. Sleeves rolled up and books cradled in his arm, he spoke to a handful of what I presumed to be college students. There were about six or seven of them gathered around him. I guessed he was either an art or history professor.

Our kids dispersed, but Eric and I moved a few steps closer to the group, hoping to hear a free lecture. Adorning the castle walls were a few pieces of framed art and several large tapestries. The man and his students were standing near a large wall hanging, and he explained that the huge thirteen-foot-wide by fifteen-foot-high silk-and-wool tapestry was an original and would have taken more than thirty years to hand weave. Then he said something that echoed not only through the Great Hall, but within my very soul.

"This tapestry is depicting King David mourning the loss of Absalom."

Then I *knew* why I was in Ireland. I knew exactly why that pop-up advertisement wouldn't go away, and I knew with one-hundred-percent certainty that God had predicted my request, and once again provided me the confirmation I needed, and that I'd asked for the very night before.

I let out an audible gasp and looked at Eric, my jaw hanging open. He too, was amazed. I didn't need to say anything for him to acknowledge my shock. I hadn't even told him I'd asked for a second confirmation the night before. The coincidence was enough to shake him.

"I know," he said. "Dat's crazy."

The professor then directed a question to his group. "Does anyone know the story of Absalom?"

The students looked at each other and shrugged their shoulders. The professor waited, hoping an answer would surface.

Surprising myself, I raised my hand and my voice to get his attention.

"I do," I proclaimed, standing a distance from his group. This was a story I knew like—well, like I'd lived it.

"Ah, yes, well somebody here knows," he said, peering at me as he leaned backwards from behind a student who was blocking his view.

I laid it all out, from the family history to position as favored son, to murdering his brother, revolting against his father, and finally hanging between Heaven and Earth in the mighty oak tree where he died, speared three times in the heart.

I felt myself going overboard, but I couldn't stop until the end. There was an uncomfortable silence, and I swallowed hard. The students turned to their professor.

"Well, um—we have a real Bible scholar here today. Thank you, ma'am," he said with a smile, his arm outstretched to acknowledge me.

I sheepishly returned the smile, knowing Absalom's story was *the only story* I'd read in the Bible, at least at that time.

I felt faint and headed for a bench. Eric stood next to me massaging my neck, waiting for me to recover while, one by one, our brood stumbled back into the room with excited stories of what the upper floors held.

Bailey plopped down beside me and, after a few minutes of uncharacteristic silence on my part, asked, "Are you all right, Mom?"

"I'll have to let you know later, Honey," I managed, staring straight ahead at the tapestry. "I'll have to let you know."

When I finally gained my composure, Eric and I ascended the winding, narrow stone staircase to the top of the turret. It was hard to focus. I felt enveloped in that familiar cloud of haziness I'd hoped to escape with a vacation. At the same time, I was elated to have the confirmation for which I'd asked.

A half-hour passed before we descended once again to the Great Hall, where the tapestry beckoned me.

"I have to get a picture with it," I told Eric as I made a beeline for the far wall where it hung.

I stood directly underneath, the bottom edge about six feet from the floor. It was an awkward arrangement, and the expression on my face made the photo even more so. I didn't know whether to look contemplative or happy. I chose contemplative. Eric snapped the picture.

"Can we try one smiling now?" he asked.

I managed a half smile. Although I was ecstatic God was still with me, my past life as Absalom didn't exactly muster feelings of pride.

As we toured the rest of the folk park, I marveled at how God had orchestrated my trip to Ireland. The confirmation was a gift beyond measure and far outweighed a frozen drink on a scorching hot beach. It was clear God had guided me across the Atlantic Ocean to receive the validation he knew I would need, a confirmation unmistakably related to Absalom. I expressed overwhelming gratitude and accepted the truth God had revealed.

I couldn't wait to get back home and give serious attention to the subject. It was hard to set it aside for the entire vacation, but I was also grateful for the opportunity our family had to spend time together exploring the history and culture of such a beautiful land. The rest of the trip was magnificent and went off without a hitch—unless you count the night we swerved to avoid an already-dead animal on the road, our car landing sideways in a ditch. We were forced to walk miles in the pitch-black darkness, afraid of cows that sounded like the hounds of the Baskervilles. I think I mentioned that our vacations are always an adventure….

Chapter Thirteen

Understanding Reincarnation

B ack home again, I devoted myself to uncovering the mysteries of reincarnation, allowing for the prerequisite knowledge that we do have souls. As with my study of angels, my objective was to garner a basic understanding of reincarnation from a religious viewpoint, and then contrast that with present-day findings culled through NDE and STE research.

Common knowledge led me first to the two main Eastern religions of Buddhism and Hinduism, in which reincarnation is a firmly held belief. I quickly determined that similar to Western religions, there are many sub-groups based on differing interpretations of holy texts and cultural influences. I aimed for the most commonly held beliefs among each religion in scouring the numerous websites that existed.

Hinduism, the main belief system of India and the world's oldest religion, comes closest to what most westerners think of when they imagine reincarnation. "The Nine Beliefs of Hinduism" found on the website for Kuai's Hindu Monastery[20], provides information on the basic underpinnings of the religion, including the concept of karma. Integral to reincarnation, karma is a reward and punishment system of re-birth (*samsa* or the *transmigration of souls*). All thoughts, deeds and actions are weighed. If one had led a good life, the next would be even better. If not, one could be demoted to a lower caste, or even return as an animal or insect if the previous life merited such an outcome. There are many gods and goddesses in Hinduism, and even they are subject to reincarnation based on the decisions of the god Vidhatta, who decides everyone's fate from lifetime to lifetime.

The ultimate goal for Hindus is *moksha*—liberation from the cycle

[20] "Nine Beliefs of Hinduism," Basics of Hinduism, Kuai's Hindu Monastery website, accessed June 12, 2018, https://www.himalayanacademy.com/readlearn/basics/nine-beliefs

of reincarnation[21]. This is accomplished by ridding one's self of *maya*, or ignorance, and living in the enlightened state, free from attachments to all things material, as well as living a life of service to mankind and the supreme god, Brahman. Only when this level is reached can one be considered enlightened, an ascended master free from the cycle of reincarnation.

In the process of incarnation, Hindus believe souls are drawn and bound to particular personalities, resulting in an embodied self, or jiva[22]. While in this state, the linga sarira (inner body, or soul), fights to overcome the desires of the physical body, which includes the animalistic body and mind. The jiva is ignorant of its true self and experiences the illusion of duality, including aversions and attractions. The resulting attachments cause one to act selfishly, as if he or she is different from everyone else. Until a soul overcomes the illusion, it cannot reach Brahman, and continues on in the never-ending cycle of creation, preservation, and finally dissolution.

Between lives, the soul lives in the highest heavenly realm to which it has progressed and continues with learning and devotions in the afterlife. Everyone will undergo many lifetimes to ultimately reach the highest level, the world of Brahman. Only then can the soul comprehend Brahman as the only *real* existence and all else as an illusion. The soul is then re-absorbed into Brahman and released from samsara, the cycle of pain and suffering that comes with reincarnation.

The cycle, believed to have begun when individual souls separated from the "undifferentiated one," will end when all is whole, or one, again. Those who have not reached Brahman by their own accord, will transform during the end of the creative cycle when all will be swept away in a great destruction.

Buddhists believe in re-birth, but technically not the transmigration of souls[23]. In Buddhist tradition a soul is not an eternal entity, but a

[21] "What Do Hindus Believe about Reincarnation?" World View, Religion, Reference, accessed June 23, 2018, https:www.reference.com/world-view/
[22] "Hinduism and the Belief in Rebirth," HinduWebsite.com, accessed June 23, 2018, https: www.hinduwebsite.com/reincarnation
[23] "On Reincarnation," Buddhist Studies, Basic Buddhism, accessed July 15, 2018, https://www.buddhanet.net/e-learning/

collection of energies constantly manipulated by the personality of the body it inhabits (what we might call "ego"). The soul therefore, has no persona or thought system that migrates. These are left behind with the inhabited body after death; or more appropriately, the ego ceases to exist. The energy collective however, can move to another body and does so based on the Buddhist idea of karma. Rather than a system of reward and punishment doled out by a god based on one's right or wrong doing via a personality, karma is an energy-based law of nature, much like gravity or magnetism. Negative energy created by negative actions will be acquired by the same collective energy unit from lifetime to lifetime. Likewise, with positive energy.

The balance of positive and negative energy carried by the unit will determine the level at which it resides while not embodied. There are said to be ten realms analogous to mental states (levels of enlightenment), which are basically levels of bliss where positive collectives will reside with like energy. The energy collective will enter a body again to try to accumulate additional positive energy and thus reach a higher level of bliss when that lifetime is over.

When an energy collective enters a body, the underlying state can either progress or go backward during that lifetime. One can control this through the eight-fold path[24], which includes right understanding, right intention, mindfulness, right speech, right action, right livelihood, right effort, and right concentration. In a nutshell, the teachings present a positive way to live in all these areas of thought and behavior.

When one understands the underlying principles of Buddhism, living by these standards becomes even more important toward achieving enlightenment. The main principle in Buddhism is that one must see true reality. Much like Hinduism, the Buddhist way to enlightenment is through the elimination of ignorance and misinformation, which leads to the end of suffering. True reality includes the recognition of impermanence—the idea that nothing is permanent. This goes for the soul—or energy collective—as well. Though energy can never be destroyed, energy collectives eventually disperse. Thus, enlightenment

[24] "The Eightfold Path: the Way to Enlightenment in Buddhism," Humanities, Religion and Spirituality, ThoughtCo, updated January 21, 2019, https://thoughtco.com/the-eightfold-path-450067

is something to be enjoyed for a short time period, both during incarnations and the states of in-between bliss.

No matter what form energy takes, whether it is in a collective or dispersed, it is everywhere, comprises everything and it cannot be extinguished. Therefore, according to Buddhism, everything is interconnected as one. Bill Bohman, Vice President of Religious Affairs at the Buddhist Temple of Chicago, illustrates this Buddhist concept of oneness on his website "That Buddha Guy"[25]:

> One of the best explanations of Oneness occurred at a Buddhist convention I attended. During the question and answer period after a seminar someone asked, "What is Oneness?" A panel member replied in a simple, understandable manner.
>
> Holding up a sheet of paper he asked, "Do you see a cloud in this paper?" No one responded. Again he asked, "Do you see a cloud in this paper?" "You must see a cloud in this paper," he continued, "because without a cloud there is no rain. Without rain there is no tree. Without a tree there is no paper." He then asked, "Do you see a steel mill? You must see a steel mill because without the mill there is no steel. Without steel there is no ax or saw to cut the tree. No tree cut down, no paper." The audience was beginning to understand his point. Chuckling he asked, "Do you see Wheaties? Loggers work hard and need a good breakfast. No loggers, no cut trees, no paper." What was the point he made? First, nothing exists independent of outside conditions. Second, no single component is more important than another. These two points, along with the idea of impermanence, are the basis of Buddhism.

While Buddhism takes a more scientific approach to the soul than Hinduism, there are elements of reincarnation within both religions that resonate with each other. Playing a major role is the need to override the ego (born through our animalistic nature) through positive living, which brings an end to suffering and moves one closer to exiting the cycle of reincarnation. Ultimately, whether Hindu or Buddhist, oneness

---

[25] "The Nature of Oneness," That Buddha Guy, accessed January 21, 2019, https://www.thatbuddhaguy.com/WhatIsOneness.html

ties everything together and is at the end of the creative cycle. There is, of course, much more complexity to both—and the various forms spawned from the main traditions—regarding reincarnation. With a basic understanding however, I moved on to the Abrahamic religions.

Mainstream Islam, Judaism, and Christianity all reject reincarnation. However, if one looks to their earliest days, reincarnation was embraced by all three. This is not too surprising considering their shared origin, relatively close geography, and core concept of monotheism. It's not hard to imagine they influenced each other's doctrine, even as they grew apart.

Followers of modern Islam are discouraged from reading their most holy book, the Koran. They are expected to take it on faith that the book contains that which its religious leaders tell them it contains. Therefore, the question of reincarnation is not outwardly debated. This likely has to do with repercussions as well—questioning doctrine can result in severe punishment.

Some references do exist, however:

> How disbelieve ye in Allah when ye were dead and He gave life to you! Then He will give you death, then life again, and then unto Him ye will return. (Koran 2:28) (https://quranx. com/2.28, Pickthall translation).

For one to be dead then brought back to life, one must have lived in the first place. The above passage indicates this happens more than once ("again").

The revered Sufi Islamic mystic Mansur Al-Hallahj, who lived between 858 A.D. and 922 A.D., wrote a poem reflective of his belief in reincarnation:

> *Like the herbage*
> *I have sprung up many a time*
> *On the banks of flowing rivers.*
> *For a hundred thousand years*
> *I have lived and worked*
> *In every sort of body.*

(http://adishakti.org/_/reincarnation_in)

At some point powerful religious leaders ousted reincarnation, likely for the same reason as Christianity: it lessened their power. With more than one life to live, followers would be less inclined toward religious perfection and obedience.

The first-century historian Flavius Josephus[26] recorded that early Jewish sects believed in reincarnation. The Pharisees, to which Saul ("Paul" after his conversion) once belonged, believed souls were "removed into other bodies" and "have power to revive and live again." The Essenes—the Jewish sect believed to have authored the Dead Sea Scrolls—were followers of Greek philosophy, including Pythagoras, who taught reincarnation, and Plato, who referenced it in his *Phaedo* and *The Republic*. According to Josephus, the Essenes believed in an immortal and pre-existent soul.

Christianity retained these beliefs as it emerged from Judaism. It is thought by many that Jesus was a student of the scholarly Essenes. Typically, one from Galilee would have been uneducated. Yet we know he surprised everyone with his knowledge and intelligence. Jesus likely spent time living and learning among the Essenes in the arid mountain cliffs overlooking the Dead Sea, in addition to learning in the Jewish temples.

In 1992, regressive hypnotherapist Dolores Cannon detailed in her book *Jesus and the Essenes*[27] her work with a woman who recalled her past life as an Essene who traveled with Jesus during his ministry. With amazing detail, the patient described Jesus' early days living and learning within her community. Cannon tested her subject throughout their sessions by periodically asking questions about the time period; questions for which verifiable answers existed, many archeologically based. The woman never failed to respond correctly.

Jesus's teaching of reincarnation is evident in the Bible, if one is open to seeing it. Following is a prominent example:

---

[26] As found and quoted from https://www.near-death.com/reincarnation/history.html.
[27] Cannon, Dolores. *Jesus and the Essenes*. Huntsville, AL: Ozark Mountain Publishing, 1992.

> As John's disciples were leaving, Jesus began to speak to the
> crowd about John.... "Then what did you go out to see? A
> prophet? Yes, I tell you, and more than a prophet. This is the
> one about whom it is written: 'I will send my messenger ahead
> of you, who will prepare your way before you ... and if you
> are willing to accept it, he is the Elijah who was to come."
> (Matt.11:7, 11:9-10, 11:14)

Jesus clearly refers to John the Baptist as being the reincarnation of
Elijah. Some have countered that Jesus meant that John the Baptist was
similar to Elijah in "spirit." Jesus said explicitly, however, for those who
are willing to accept it, that he *was* Elijah.

In *Why Jesus Taught Reincarnation* (referenced earlier), author
Herbert Bruce Puryear makes an interesting argument in support of
Jesus' acknowledgement of reincarnation. In John 3:7, Jesus spoke
to Nicodemus, saying "Ye must be born again." This has oft been
interpreted as meaning one must be re-born in spirit to be saved. When
the history is taken into account, Puryear notes, it's clear Jesus is referring
to re-birth of the spirit into other bodies.

> There was a man of the Pharisees, named Nicodemus, a ruler
> of the Jews. (John 3:1)

Nicodemus's background sets the stage for Jesus's teaching. Being a
Pharisee, Nicodemus believed in reincarnation. According to Josephus,
the Pharisees believed in an immortal soul, a spirit life, and the ability
for souls of the virtuous to migrate into other bodies. They also believed
in the Old Testament's promise that Elijah and the Messiah were both
to come again. The conversation between Nicodemus and Jesus begins:

> The same came to Jesus by night, and said unto him, "Rabbi,
> we know that thou art a teacher come from God: for no man
> can do these miracles that thou doest, except God be with him."

> Jesus answered and said unto him, "Verily, verily, I say unto
> thee, except a man be born again, he cannot see the kingdom
> of God." (John 3:2–3)

Nowhere in these passages does Nicodemus or Jesus speak of

being saved. In fact, the errant interpretation has Jesus ignoring what Nicodemus said, apparently going on to speak of something unrelated to the observation.

It is more logical to interpret Nicodemus's statement as an expression of wonderment. He is in awe that Jesus *must* be one of the promised ones to come (Elijah, the Messiah, or another prophet), and therefore has already been in God's presence in the "kingdom of God." Jesus, knowing Nicodemus was a Pharisee, responded in accordance to his pupil's understanding. Rather than assuming Jesus ignores Nicodemus' observation, his response can be taken as an affirmation that all men must be born again in order to see God in God's kingdom. Nicodemus continues the conversation:

> Nicodemus saith unto him, "How can a man be born when he is old? Can he enter the second time into his mother's womb, and be born?" (John 3:4)

At first glance, this question makes Nicodemus seem like a wide-eyed child asking a silly question. In fact, it is a fair and intelligent question based on the Pharisees' belief that a soul, upon the death of its body, can inhabit another adult body if their *mitsvah* (earthly mission) had not been completed. Nicodemus would have been familiar with this version of soul migration, but apparently did not understand the mechanics of being born again. Jesus responds to his question:

> Jesus answered, "Verily, verily I say unto thee, except a man be born of water and of the Spirit, he cannot enter in to the kingdom of God." (John 3:5)

This is usually interpreted as the need to be baptized and saved. My own interpretation of this, keeping Nicodemus' understanding in mind, is that the passage might also refer to two different types of water. "Born of water," could refer to when a woman's water breaks and she gives birth, or it could refer to the flowing river of life. Both allude to the mechanics of *how* life is given. I have also noticed that "born of water" comes before being born of "spirit." This order reflects the mechanics of reincarnation. One must go through the cycle of birth (water) many times before they can be "born of the spirit," as was Jesus, meaning he had evolved to the highest state possible and "was come from God (the highest state, the "kingdom of God").

Being "baptized" and "saved" are both symbolic gestures. My assessment is that Jesus, having been sinless, would have had no need to be baptized, but felt it "proper" to "fulfill all righteousness" (Matt. 3:13-15). Proper, but not necessary. Why? So *all* can reach ascension. Baptism is a reminder to work toward a righteous spirit, the mechanics of which are re-birth.

Being "saved" in a traditional sense is also a symbolic ritual created by man. Nowhere in the Bible does it mandate one must confess Jesus as their savior. Instead, one must save himself by going through the *suffering* that lifetimes afford. As discussed in the chapter on suffering, it is not punishment for sin, but an opportunity to learn lessons of love so a soul may eventually remember its true identity as sinless and one with God. There are many counter arguments to this, as Jesus said many things that could be interpreted one way or another. This is one viewpoint.

While mainstream Judaism and Christianity have rejected reincarnation, some today still believe it to be a truth of our existence, including Hasidic Jews, Kabbalists and some Christians. In a 2009 survey by Pew Forum[28], twenty-five percent of otherwise mainstream Christians said they believe in reincarnation. An online article that first appeared in the *New York Times*[29] the following year reported on the growing trend, with nearly a quarter of Americans convinced it is a real phenomenon.

NDE research shines new light on reincarnation. Thousands of NDE testimonies include being shown or told about past lives. New material is being captured daily, thanks to technology that allows individuals to easily share their experiences with researches and like communities via the internet; and to individuals and organizations who are making spiritually-oriented study credible.

---

[28] www.americamagazine.org/faith/2015/10/21/25-percent-us-christians-believe-reincarnation-whats-wrong-picture

[29] www.personalityspirituality.net/2010/09/05/western-belief-in-reincarnation-on-the-increase/

The International Association for Near-Death Studies (IANDS.org) is one such group. One of its most important undertakings has been the collection of first-hand NDE accounts. Many researchers have culled verifiable subjects from these files for their studies (verifiable meaning proof of clinical death). Other organizations include The Near-Death Experience Research Foundation (NDERF.org) and NEAR-DEATH. com. Following are examples from these sites of near-death experiences where individuals were told by spirit beings (often angels or Jesus), about reincarnation:

> I was told that I had a long history of past lives filled with anger, aggression and hate.... We reincarnate to learn different things ... impossible in a single lifetime. (NDERF.org, NDE 4251)

> There was a review of my life in this body, and also my past lives. I was the judge as to the benefit and value of each experience ... [which] contributed to an end result. (NDERF.org, NDE 3637)

> I also knew that if I didn't come back at this time, in this body, I would return to the Earth school in another body, to finish what I was here to do. Before the experience, I didn't believe or disbelieve in reincarnation. Now I am sure that I have had many reincarnations. (NDERF.org, NDE 727)

> I was given the choice of remaining with the light, provided I return later to the physical world and experience all that brought me to the point of shooting myself, or I could return now and pick up my life where it was. (*Lessons from the Light*[30], NDE of Sandi Rogers)

It's easy to believe in reincarnation when you've been told about or shown your past lives by a divine being, but even those experiencers who weren't told explicitly of it typically have become believers. Amber Wells, in her thesis as a student at the University of Connecticut in 1993,

---

[30] Rogers, Sandra. *Lessons from the Light. Insights from a Journey to the Other Side.* Grand Rapids, MI: Grand Central Publishing, 2009.

under the tutelage of seasoned NDE research pioneer Dr. Kenneth Ring, points out:

> Research has indicated that following a near-death experience (NDE), experiencers tend to exhibit a significant shift in their beliefs on a wide range of subjects, including an increased acceptance of others, a significantly greater belief in life after death, and a decreased emphasis on material success (Atwater, 1988; Flynn, 1986; Grey, 1985; Morse and Perry, 1992; Ring, 1984, 1992; Sutherland, 1992). These belief changes have also included a general tendency toward an increased openness to the idea of reincarnation (Gallup and Proctor, 1982; Ring, 1980, 1984, 1992; Sutherland, 1992). (near-death.com/reincarnation/research/kenneth-ring.html)

In her study, 70% of NDE subjects said they believed in reincarnation, compared to only 23% of the general population in a U.S. Gallup poll cited in the study. This may be due to another phenomenon of the NDE, reported as a *knowing* of all information that exists past, present, and future. Some have explained this as tapping into the *one mind* or the *Christ consciousness.*

It is commonly believed in spiritual circles that all past-life memories are contained within the Akashic Records. Although individuals might recall their own past lives, the records are part of the collective consciousness, the one mind. This explains how a past-life review is possible. When these occur, guides que up on a large screen (or something similar) what appears as a movie of the new arrival's life. If it helps them progress, sometimes a past life (sometimes multiple lives) is shown in an effort to break patterns of repetition.

Many experiencers have noted being immersed in the action and able to experience others' feelings. Logically, not only is the experiencer's record accessed, but so too are the records of those with whom he or she has interacted.

The Akashic records can be accessed by earthly helpers such as past-life regression therapists and spiritual counsellors. A year after my STEs, I visited Doris Eliana Cohen, Ph.D. Dr. Cohen served as a clinical psychologist and psychotherapist for more than thirty years when she discovered her ability to communicate with spirit guides. It was Dr. Cohen who first told me of the Akashic records, pointing out that access is limited to records pertinent to those lessons intended to be learned in the current life.

I shared the revelation of my past life as Absalom before Dr. Cohen attempted to access my records. I was not there to test her, but to learn. She was able to uncover several lifetimes I had lived. In one, I had been a male Scottish warrior and Bailey my young male protégé. We'd become friends, and I was harder on him than the rest, not wanting to lose him in battle. Whether I did lose him was not clear, but the juxtaposition with my current life reflected my constant worry over Bailey getting hurt or injured.

While a mother's concern for a daughter's safety isn't unusual, when Dr. Cohen told me about this past life, I suddenly remembered a recurring dream I'd had since Bailey was young where she proudly brought me a severed head in a basket. It was a disturbing dream and I couldn't figure out what my subconscious mind was telling me. It makes perfect sense now. I believe I was conflicted within myself—and thereby causing my daughter to be conflicted—by encouraging her to take risks and not be afraid, but at the same time constantly cautioning her about dangers and pitfalls.

In her book, *Repetition, Past Lives, Life and Rebirth*[31], Dr. Cohen explains how understanding past lives can lead to healing in the current life. Once negative, repetitive behavior is identified, patients can examine their past lives to see how and why particular behaviors developed, which is the first step toward change. In her book, Dr. Cohen presents ways individuals can help themselves on the journey of discovery and healing, including the seven steps of rebirth, and the four steps of joy.

In *Many Lives, Many Masters*[32], Brian L. Weiss, M.D. recounts the journey of one such patient—a journey so profound and unexpected it propelled him as a therapist into an entirely new area of healing. He is

---

[31] Cohen, Doris Eliana, PH.D., *Repetition. Past Lives, Life, and Rebirth*. New York: Hay House, 2008.
[32] Weiss, Brian L., M.D., *Many Lives, Many Masters*. New York: Simon & Schuster, Inc., 1988.

known today for his pioneering work in past-life regression therapy, and it all began with his twenty-seven-year old patient, Catherine.

Catherine had come to Dr. Weiss for help with anxiety, panic attacks and phobias. When no traditional modalities helped, he turned to hypnosis to regress Catherine to her childhood so they might uncover hidden reasons behind her disorders. To his surprise, he soon found Catherine speaking under hypnosis of past lives and providing information from spirit entities. In one session, Catherine regressed to an in-between state after reliving a death in a past life. There, she realized she had not met the goals of that life:

> I should have been more forgiving, but I wasn't. I did not forgive the wrongs that people did to me, and I should have. I didn't forgive the wrongs. I held them inside, and I harbored them for many years.

Had Catherine learned to forgive in previous lifetimes, her current life may have been easier. Instead, she continued to be hurt in relationships, but couldn't understand why. Now, it became apparent that the hurt people caused her were, reversely, opportunities for her to practice and learn forgiveness. In the same session, she shared information spirits of ascended masters told her:

> What plane we go to depends upon how far we've progressed.... Only we can rid ourselves...of the bad habits that we accumulate when we are in a physical state. The Masters cannot do that for us.... When you decide that you are strong enough to master the external problems, then you will no longer have them in your next life.

As Catherine confronted the reasons for her anxieties, her condition improved until she no longer needed therapy.

Many near-death experiencers remember learning the same thing on the other side—that problems in their current life are not the result of karma, but of their own planning. Judgement, far from being passed on us by God, is more of an assessment of how well (or not) one learned the lessons they planned for themselves.

In Dr. Eben Alexander's third book, *Living in a Mindful Universe*[33], he relates the story of Cynthia, a forty-two-year-old woman who underwent hypnosis in an effort to overcome her issues of low self-esteem and body image. She had been mocked her entire life by other children and one especially cruel uncle for her unappealing looks and big nose. Her therapist guided her to the "in-between time" after her previous life and prior to her current life:

> I was a very beautiful and tall woman. It was an elegant life, but I was actually rather vein. Oh, I was really awful. I felt I was so much better than everyone else.... This is very hard for me to see. How could I have been so arrogant? ...I ridiculed and made fun of others who were not so beautiful. I was actually, well, really mean. I am not at all like that today. How could I have behaved in such a way?

Cynthia's therapist probed further leading her to an "in-between" time where she assessed her growth:

> I certainly don't want to be beautiful (in my next life). I want to find out what it is like to be made fun of. I want to be teased and ridiculed.... Maybe a big nose would be good...? I want to be teased so I really know how it feels and never act this way again.

Generally, we plan our own lives and lessons in conjunction with other souls to whom we are close (termed a soul family). Someone who was one's mother in a past life might return in a future life as a sister or friend. The possibilities are endless. Ironically, the people in our lives who seem to present us with the most challenges, are those who love us the most and help us to create the learning opportunities we need.

In Dr. Alexander's example, Cynthia was terrified when she first saw her uncle in Heaven, as he had been especially cruel to her. To her surprise, he expressed an overwhelming love toward her and explained that his role had been one of the most difficult things he'd ever done for her. In planning their lifetimes together, Cynthia had made him

---

[33] Alexander, Eben, M.D., and Newell, Karen, *Living in a Mindful Universe. A Neurosurgeon's Journey into the Heart of Consciousness*. U.S.A.: Rodale Wellness, 2017.

promise to tease and hurt her so she could overcome her tendency to tease and hurt others.

Dr. Weiss's patient, Catherine, alluded to this same system. She referred to it as paying debts—entering a lifetime with another soul to play a difficult role, returning a favor for them having done the same in an earlier lifetime.

Dr. Alexander encourages us to examine our lives from this perspective:

> Consider all the relationship issues many of us have endured, whether as parent-child, husband-wife, or boss-employee. This school of thought implies we make such plans together, knowingly and with love.... It is not necessary to fully accept it as truth. Simply ask yourself "What if it is true?" Then look back on specific life events, especially those that were catalysts for change, and contemplate, "Why might I have planned that?" or "Did something useful result?" Pay attention to your answers, and trust your intuitions.

The suffering we plan for ourselves can be enormous. Suzanne Giesemann, a gifted evidential medium who channels her spirit guides, has been told by them that those on the other side consider humans the bravest of souls! I concur.

According to emerging research, reincarnation might not be linear as we perceive it, but rather multi-dimensional, with many lives going on simultaneously in different realms and universes. Add to this, the idea that our *core* soul is always present in the spiritual world. It sends aspects of itself into different physical realms for different experiences. Often termed *our higher self*, it acts as our intuition and the voice in our head that gives us direction, as if watching all the action from a higher vantage point.

This concept might explain why Ben Breedlove (whose story sparked my STEs) encountered Kid Cudi in his NDE, even though Kid Cudi was, and is still, alive. Others have reported seeing still-living loved ones in their NDEs as well:

> One of them asked me to think about something I really desired ... suddenly I had an urge for a piece of my mother's

famous homemade chocolate cake with her special fudge frosting. As soon as I thought of the cake, my earthly mother was handing me the biggest piece of dark chocolate cake I had ever seen.... Although she appeared there with us, I knew some part of her was still back on Earth because she had not died yet. My guess was that she was probably asleep, dreaming of lovingly making her son a piece of her divine chocolate cake. (NDERF.org, NDE 7743)

While reincarnation cannot yet be proven, the overwhelming number of people who remember past lives either through regression therapy, near-death experience, or spontaneous knowing, coupled with findings by credible researchers, point to its reality. Though there is subtle variation in theory, the consensus among the spiritually-minded is that it is a mechanism for growth and learning, spread over many lifetimes and throughout many realms of existence. Because this points to evolution, there is clearly something we are evolving toward, and that seems to be the purest form of energy, which is love, which is God.

Certainly, there is more to learn about reincarnation. I suspect we have only touched the tip of the iceberg; but I also suspect that learning will come quickly now that human awareness is shifting.

Also shifting as I learned about reincarnation, was my view of Absalom. I understood that he was more than the negative traits that defined him forever in the annals of history. He was dimensional—a soul whose lessons were my own, and from whose turmoil I have benefited. If my conclusions regarding reincarnation are correct, then my soul has come a long way in just 3,000 short years—though I'm certain I still have a long way to go.

CHAPTER FOURTEEN

CONFIRMATION III, THE CLEVELAND MUSEUM OF ART

M y conclusions felt right, but I couldn't be sure they were correct. It was a self-study crash course after all. Even if I'd been taught about reincarnation by the world's most revered gurus, I likely would have second-guessed the teachings. I kept reminding myself that just a few short months ago I was a die-hard agnostic. There was only one place I could turn for answers, so—you guessed it, I asked God for yet *another* confirmation.

This time I didn't question whether I had been Absalom. I simply needed to know that my understanding of reincarnation was correct, so any future study of my soul's path would be grounded in truth. It was a gutsy move, I know, but God had not indicated to me that he didn't appreciate my gumption. Incidentally, years later when telling my story to a friend, she pointed out that in the Bible, whenever God gives someone a message or confirmation, he usually does so three times. I guess humans are a hard-headed lot!

It was a breezy, overcast Sunday, and my sister and I had planned to go to the Cleveland Flea, an indoor flea market held in downtown Cleveland once a year. Neither of us had ever been but we'd talked many times about going, and I was excited to have my sister help me pick out some antique or eclectic items for my house. She has a great eye for decorating and sees treasures in things I wouldn't have picked up in a million years. I pulled into the driveway of her quaint cottage in Bay Village, and we took her car into the city, a fifteen-minute drive when traffic is light.

Once off the highway, we meandered down several side streets before pulling into an unkempt back parking lot that was actually a conglomerate of smaller lots surrounded on the outer perimeter by buildings a few stories high with peeling paint and naked vines crawling up the sides. I easily spotted the back entrance to the flea market—a white brick building with a string of blinking red Christmas lights outlining the glass door. As we arrived it began to drizzle and a line was forming at the door, so we decided to wait a few minutes until it cleared up. That proved to be a mistake because when we did get in line it had slowed to a crawl. In the meantime, it was getting colder and seemed like forever before we got near the front of the line. Finally, there were only a few people ahead of us when, to our horror, a portly security guard, baton in hand, stuck his head out and announced no one else could enter.

Moans and groans rose up from those behind us, and I found myself nearly shouting at the guy.

"We waited all this time in the cold, and now you tell us we can't come in? Not even a few more people at the front of the line here?" I gestured to the two women ahead of me with a baby in a stroller and three toddlers in tow.

The guard thumped his billy club into his open hand, stressing certain words. "The FIRE marshal ordered the entrance LOCKED due to OVER CROWDING. We can't let ANYONE ELSE IN until we get an ALL CLEAR," he instructed.

"How long?" the woman in front pleaded, grabbing her fleeing five-year-old by the back of his collar.

"No telling. It could be SEVERAL HOURS," he thumped.

After more people joined our effort to convince the guard to *do something*, we realized we couldn't change the situation.

Deflated, my sister and I got back in the car and drove around to see what else we could possibly do downtown on a rainy Sunday. Nothing seemed appealing due to the drizzle, but we stopped at an Italian food market and sampled some cheese and cannoli. That killed ten minutes.

Back in the car, I suggested we visit my old haunt, the natural history museum. I knew it was a long shot though, because my sister wasn't into old bones.

She drew out a long "Nah," as I saw an idea spark to life in her eyes.

"But we could go to the art museum!" she said, adding that her boss was a new board member there.

Neither of us was particularly into art, but we never minded exploring outside our usual interests. Over the preceding five years, I'd been to several prominent art museums because of my step daughter's blossoming interest in the field, but I couldn't remember the last time I'd been to The Cleveland Museum of Art.

"Sounds like a plan," I agreed, and off we went.

Inside, our voices echoed off the smooth, white, marble floors, walls, and ceilings. We decided our plan was not to have a plan, but to wander wherever we wanted. We took a quick look around on the first floor. There were a few pieces of art on display in the atrium, but it mostly housed the gift shop and restaurant, so we made our way to the escalator and ascended to the second floor.

Upstairs, my sister went right and I went left. I flung open one of the tall glass double doors and entered a large gallery. I hadn't paid attention to any signage, so I didn't know anything about the collection. The first painting on display was a large three-foot-high by four-foot-wide canvas. A tall, tan-skinned man with short, greying black hair and matching long beard sat pensively overlooking a wall toward an arid mountain landscape, his firsts curled as if in despair. I stood back and observed, channeling my inner artist. I'd never developed a scholarly approach to art, so I went with a straight layman's interpretation.

The colors were somber, a mix of black, deep reds, and golds. Grey, swirling clouds blocked an evening sun. I moved closer for clues as to what the man was thinking. On the ground at his feet lay a golden crown resting on its side, as if he had pulled it off his head and let it slip from his fingers. His stately chair sat atop a Persian rug, and a golden hoop hung from his right ear.

He was clearly royalty, and clearly distraught, I discerned proudly, ready to move on to the next painting.

Before doing so however, I took a step forward, leaned in, and squinted at the title placard on the wall:

"David Mourning the Loss of Absalom"

I gasped and backed away, immediately aware this was the third confirmation for which I'd been asking. As in Ireland, God used art specifically referencing Absalom so there was no mistaking the communique.

I retrieved my reading glasses from my purse and read the rest of the information. It was painted by Lord Frederic Leighton of Stretton, England, 1830-1896. There was an accompanying quote:

David: "Oh, that I had the Wings of a Dove! For then I would fly away and be at rest."

He had truly loved Absalom, despite his son's rebellious ways. I stared at the man in the painting, knowing the image had been created in the artist's mind, but still overwhelmed that I was in some way looking at my father from a time long since passed. The magnitude of his love was apparent and transcended time.

Suddenly, I realized something that hadn't occurred to me before. I understood that my soul's journey reflected a much bigger picture. No matter how much we rebel against our father—God, our creator—he will love us unconditionally, and he is awaiting our return. Like the prodigal son, I knew I had been forgiven by David and God, though it may have taken me 3,000 years to come to this realization. God, who captioned David as one after his own heart will eventually welcome all his wayward children home again.

I don't know how long I sat on the bench in front of the painting but eventually I noticed my sister outside the glass door standing in the distance, looking for me. She'd apparently been through an entire exhibit, while I hadn't gotten beyond one painting. Excitedly, I jumped up from the bench, propped the door open and motioned for her to come over.

"You have to see this," I said a little too loudly, my words bouncing off the walls. Besides Eric and Bailey, the only others I'd told about my experiences at that time were my step-mother, my dad, and my sister. I hadn't told my sister I'd been asking for another confirmation, though. In fact, I had forgotten about it, so I wasn't on the lookout for a sign. In retrospect, I should have known it was coming when our plans to visit the Cleveland Flea were unexpectedly averted by order of the fire marshal. Remember my tropical beach vacation plans? There's a lesson for all here. When your best laid plans go awry, go with the flow. There's most likely an unseen reason.

With trepidation I pointed out the painting to my sister. I didn't know if she believed in the divine nature of my experiences, but I was too overjoyed not to share. She didn't say much, but shot me that older sister look that says *you're off your rocker.*

A couple of hours later, we were done with art. Before leaving the museum, I felt compelled to take a quick look around the gift shop despite my sister's insistence on leaving. I didn't plan on buying anything, but something caught my eye and I had to have it. Of all the paintings on display, the museum had selected a small handful to reproduce on postcards. I bought four, all the same: Leighton's masterpiece, *"David."* I considered it an early Christmas present from God.

CHAPTER FIFTEEN

VOICE OF GOD

After having gone through such miraculous experiences, I had become a ninety-nine-percent, *almost* full-on believer. Doubt only came around once in a blue moon, and visits were shorter. I tried to remedy the residual one percent by continuing to read and study as much as possible. I'd even started attending church again regularly for the first time since childhood. I wanted desperately to maintain my extraordinary connection with God.

Eric had never been the church-going type and spending Sundays apart during our already short weekends was not appealing, so I devised a plan to pique his interest in us joining a church together. I targeted local non-denominational churches, presuming one with no affiliation would equate to a more open mindset.

For our twelfth anniversary we had planned a trip to Hawaii, made possible by one of those resort timeshare schemes and air miles from Eric's frequent travel rewards. It would be the honeymoon we'd never taken. My idea was to surprise him the day before our departure with a ceremony to renew our wedding vows. After calling a few churches in the area, I found one where the pastor was available on the designated day and willing to re-marry us without a lot of hoopla. We only had to show up and get hitched!

The morning of the ceremony, I secretly placed on the kitchen counter a box wrapped in shiny white wedding paper, along with a card. Eric, not too surprised considering our impending trip, opened the envelope first.

"Marry Me?" I'd written inside the card. Then he *was* surprised.

He unwrapped the gift—two champagne flutes with silver stems adorned with interlocking hearts and crystal studs. On the glass I'd had engraved "Nancy & Eric," with two overlapping hearts on the next line and "Always and Forever" underneath the hearts.

"For after the ceremony," I smiled.

I told him I'd arranged an intimate renewal of our vows with just the two of us and a pastor, and there wasn't a thing he needed to do or worry about, but he looked apprehensive.

I raised my eyebrow. "You *do* want to marry me, don't you?"

He laughed and pulled me into a bear hug.

"It's not for nothing dat I'm here. And I would marry you a million times over," he said kissing my forehead.

"Well, good," I responded. "Because everything's booked, and you're not getting out of it," I said.

He pulled the champagne glasses from their foam insert, rinsed them in the sink, and poured a swallow of orange juice into each.

"Dare's just one little problem," he said, raising his glass.

"I'm not sure I want to clink until I know how little, 'little' is," I said, pulling my glass back.

"I forgot to tell you, I have a rood canal today."

"You're kidding," I said. "You booked a root canal the day before our vacation?"

I shouldn't have been surprised because Eric is one who plows through things, come what may.

"Dat's when da dentist could do it. I didn't know I get married today," he laughed.

"Well what time is your *rooood* canal?" I asked, setting my glass on the counter, about to give up.

"One o'clock. Dir-teen hundred," he declared using his military matter-of-factness to convey that the appointment was firm and he was sticking to it.

"Okay, I think we can make that work," I said. "The ceremony is at ten. I planned to take pictures afterward, then we have a reservation for lunch at Dakota's, but I can cancel that."

Relieved, I picked up my glass and we clinked to our future years together.

"Cheers," I said.

"Probst."

The ceremony consisted of the two of us and the pastor, with a few of the congregation milling around doing unrelated chores. The church was idyllic: a small, white chapel in a quaint pastoral setting fifteen minutes from our home. Pastor Gillespie had an easygoing manner and encouraged us to attend services once we were back from our trip. It was just the invite I'd hoped to receive. Eric is a social butterfly, and I knew he'd be willing to visit again if asked.

We quickly grew to love The Church at Sunny Dale, both the people and the pastor. While Bible-based, Pastor Gillespie was open minded and had a unique way of engaging people, prompting them to interpret scripture for themselves. He often quipped, "If that's what you believe," making it clear everyone had free will to interpret the Bible from their hearts and their unique perspectives. I liked that.

Considering I chose Sunny Dale because it was the only non-denominational church available when we needed it, I think God had a hand in guiding me there. I whole-heartedly believe my non-adherence to doctrine is why, in part, I had my STEs. To accept God had communicated with me, I didn't need to overcome doctrine that might have been hammered into my psyche. No, I had only to get past my own ego and bent toward materialistic science.

It was nearly a year after my STEs and about six months since we started attending Sunny Dale before I divulged my story to Pastor Gillespie. I was certainly learning a lot from his sermons, but I hadn't yet attempted to get an opinion on my STEs from anyone I assumed was closer to God than me—the reason that drove me back to church in the first place.

A few days before Thanksgiving, Eric and I helped other church members ladle out bowls of soup for those in need during Sunny Dale's annual Thanksgiving Soup Kitchen. Afterwards, guests carried out turkeys and all the trimmings necessary to prepare their own holiday meals at home. When the event wound down I took my chance, telling Pastor Gillespie I wanted to share something with him. As the last few people exited the community room, he grabbed a bottle of red wine and three glasses, correctly sensing a long story.

I gingerly laid it all out, trying to be as calm and collected as possible. Eric jumped in occasionally only to clarify a point. The pastor listened intently, but reserved his comments. When I finally finished, there was silence. I wasn't sure he realized I'd come to the end of my story, or if he was stupefied beyond words. I broke the silence.

"What do you make of all this?" I asked.

"I've heard things like this before," he started slowly. "From people who were *bat-shit-crazy!*"

Ouch, that stung. For a moment I regretted opening my mouth, then he continued.

"But I don't think you're crazy. I think maybe you have a calling," he said.

It had gotten dark outside and the bottle was empty. He rose from the table and Eric and I followed his cue. He commented about Absalom's life, but nothing further about the miraculous nature of my experiences. It was late, and he needed to get home—and quite possibly away from me. I thought we might talk another day about this calling thing, so we said goodnight and I was satisfied for the time being just not to be bat-shit-crazy.

We never did talk about it again. To be fair, I never asked. Similar scenarios occurred over the next few years when I sought input from other clergy at other churches. Sadly, some were compelled to put a negative spin on what I considered sacred. I simply couldn't understand how my experiences could be "bad" when they drew me to God. Didn't Jesus say in Luke 11:18, "If Satan also be divided against himself, how can his kingdom stand?" Ultimately, I realized that what I would do about my experiences and the messages I received, was between me and God.

Don't think I didn't investigate counter-arguments for why my STEs may have occurred—brain science and all that. The underlying problem with neuro nay-sayers is they practice purely physical science. They do not acknowledge spiritual experiences as anything more than hallucination. How can you study something you don't acknowledge exists? It's a conundrum.

Dr. Eben Alexander, whom I referenced earlier, is turning the tables on his medical colleagues' thinking. In *Living in a Mindful Universe*, he narrows the gap between spirituality and science with information culled from both his medical training, NDEs—including his own—and the study of consciousness. There are many others like him working to change the current paradigm. Still, it remains an emerging field.

Eventually, I came to the conclusion that I had to live with my doubt.

Why shouldn't I? Most people do. I accepted it as the antagonist moving me forward on my journey. I didn't necessarily like that I couldn't commit one hundred percent to my belief in God, but I counted my blessings knowing I had been given more than most.

What I forgot is that God doesn't work on the clock. My core STEs ended after I received the last confirmation at the art museum, and though I tried hard to re-connect with God in the profound manner I'd gotten accustomed to, my efforts were futile.

Nearly three years later, Eric and I were headed for a new life in New Jersey. I hated to leave our old house in Ohio where angels had tread, but as I learned from Buddha's teachings, nothing is permanent. I tried to look at the bright side—at least Bailey had finished high school and was off to college, so the change didn't impact her. At the same time, Eric was excited to pursue new challenges in his career, so at forty-seven years old I left all I knew behind for whatever God had in store for me.

For the first year and a half, we lived in a small apartment about ten miles from where our new home was being built. Much of south Jersey is rural, so even the towns and small cities felt pastoral compared to where we'd come from in northeast Ohio. We had a cozy second floor unit with large windows and a sliding glass door that opened to a small balcony overlooking an open field with horses and a big red barn in the distance. I loved waking up to roosters crowing on the neighboring farm. Rent was definitely more than we'd wanted to pay, but Eric chose the apartment on his own and wanted me to feel as comfortable as possible. I'd suddenly been hit with so many changes, he worried I'd be depressed.

Truth be told, I was busier than ever and didn't have time to be sad. With Eric required to be in an office now when not on a business trip, and his travel schedule still heavy, the responsibility of making decisions about the house fell mostly to me. In addition, because we were building our home, I spent time sourcing and negotiating with contractors for things like septic systems and kitchen cabinets. It wasn't easy being new in town, with no one to give me advice or references. It seemed I was on the phone or running back and forth between the apartment, our property, and the builder's office from dawn to dusk on most days.

I did manage to enjoy some quiet time however, especially when

Eric was away and I was alone in the evenings. On one occasion I ventured out to a shopping area I'd not been to before. I was pleased to find a Barnes and Noble, especially because bookstores were on their way out thanks to e-readers like Kindles and Nooks. I appreciated the environmental benefits and the ability to carry hundreds of books in one space-saving device, but I still loved browsing the shelves and flipping through pages.

My interest in all things spiritual had not waned and I knew right where to go—the hippie section. I had a developing interest in meditation so I picked out a couple publications with "beginner" in the title. I found a few more books that piqued my interest and I added them to my pile then headed to checkout.

I delved into the introductions of all six books when I got home, settling on one for my evening's companionship. When it got too dark to continue reading on the patio, I headed inside and readied for bed. I stole Eric's pillow since he wasn't home, propped it up over mine, and made myself a comfy backrest so I could read a bit more before turning out the light. While the book in hand wasn't about reincarnation, the author touched on it. She suggested most people had lived hundreds, if not thousands, of lives. I thought that if reincarnation is how we learn— and there is almost unlimited learning to be done—then her estimate made sense. I was too tired to give it any more thought than that.

I set the book on my nightstand, turned off the lamp, and tossed Eric's pillow back onto his side of the bed. Settling in, I said a quick prayer, then nonchalantly—just as I had first asked God about reincarnation—I posed a question:

—And God, I know reincarnation is real and that I lived as Absalom. But how many times have I lived? I asked.

I didn't expect an answer. God had stopped interacting with me in such an overt manner after that day in the Cleveland art museum. I drifted off into a deep sleep until morning came.

Normally, I transition from sleep to wakefulness as everyone else does, via a slow powering-up of the body and mind that makes one progressively more aware as sleep nears the end of its cycle. When I first open my eyes, I feel groggy because the process is still taking place.

Not on this particular morning. On this morning, I went from being in a deep sleep to being fully awake instantly. It was the same as when I instantly awakened when Jesus visited, and again when I was given the name "Absalom," only this time it was my physical body that awoke. From a dreamless void, I suddenly opened my eyes—my biological eyes. I rolled over in bed and pushed my upper torso up on my outstretched arms. Yoga instructors would call this the up-dog position. I have no idea why I did this, it wasn't a typical move for me. I think I did so of my own volition, but one never knows.

As I lifted my chin, I noticed bright golden sunshine on the walls. Suddenly, approximately a foot behind me to the left, level with my ear, I heard an *audible voice* as clear as a bell, say:

"There are seven in the ground."

There is no other way to say this, except that God *audibly spoke to me*. I looked back over my left shoulder, but no one was there. I wasn't scared at all. On the contrary, I felt overjoyed God was back (of course, he'd never really left), and I was beyond thrilled to have had the most direct contact I'd experienced so far! I did not feel compelled to say anything in response. I was elated, and all I could do was smile. I felt so extremely close to God at that moment that words fail to describe it.

I sat on the edge of the bed basking in the sunlight pouring into the room. I knew I'd have to unpack the answer, but I chose to simply enjoy the sacredness of the moment for as long as possible. What was immediately clear was God had given me far more than an answer to my question. His audible response had wiped from my egocentric brain, all remaining doubt. Up until that point, I'd been inching toward God, accepting little-by-little as divine, the strange "coincidences" I'd experienced. Now, God revealed himself to me through purely human sensory perception—in this case, hearing. I heard what I heard, of that I've never been more certain. God's voice was crystal clear, but neither a whisper nor a shout. It was neither deep nor high-pitched, nor male or female. It was not monotone nor highly inflective. It was…perfect for the occasion.

When I reflected on the answer, it made me laugh to know God understood me so well. His answer was clever and anticipatory. Rather than giving me a number, like "seven" or "eight," God had responded in the most precise manner possible, while also leaving no room for confusion. "There are seven in the ground" infers there have been seven *bodies* before my current body, which of course is not in the ground yet. I thought about how I'd asked my question, "How many times have I lived?" If God had answered with a simple number, I would have eventually wondered whether that number included me, or just my prior lives. My question left room for error. God's answer had not. This was the *coup de grace* of my journey.

Now I am ready and willing with a fully committed heart to do whatever it is God has in store for me. Sharing my story is the just the beginning.

CHAPTER 16, CONCLUSION

THE GRANDER LESSON AND
FOUR HABITS OF LOVE

T he messages given to me collectively convey a part of God's grand plan for humanity, and the overarching lesson is that we are all *one*. Our souls are a part of God and can never be extinguished. At some point, we, as God's children, moved away from God and the farther we went, the more we believed in our existence only as separate beings. In reality, we are forever connected. Some have observed humanity as being "the body of Christ," and this is true if you think of Christ as the Christ consciousness, the one mind, or the all-pervasive source of all that is.

More so, it is the soul, not the body, to which God granted eternal existence, being inseparable from himself. Man is indeed appointed to live and die once (Hebrews 9:27), but the *soul* continues to learn lessons to make its way back to pure source, which is pure love, which is God. In our quest to purify our souls, we must learn unconditional love. This is impossible in one lifetime, therefore God implemented reincarnation. Through this mechanism, our souls return to Earth lifetime after lifetime to learn love—to know God.

> Love is patient, love is kind. It does not envy, it does not boast,
> it is not proud. It does not dishonor others, it is not self-seeking,
> it is not easily angered, it keeps no record of wrongs. Love does
> not delight in evil but rejoices with the truth. It always protects,
> always trusts, always hopes, always perseveres. (1 Cor. 13:4-9)

Earth is a world of opposites, making it the perfect environment for humans to encounter challenges. These challenges are the cause of suffering, and suffering offers the opportunity to choose and learn love. It is not a new notion, but put succinctly, Earth is a school. For sure, it is a playground as well with all its beauty to explore and adventures to undertake. No matter what one is doing however, whether playing or working or interacting in some other way, the opportunity to practice love is always present.

I received the amazing gift of knowledge. God then confirmed my understanding was correct, that our souls are evolving. I can look at the life of Absalom and compare it to my current life and see how far I've come. I believe humanity has progressed as a whole. It's not a coincidence that alongside technological advances we have experienced a big leap forward in spiritual evolution. As the world shrinks via means of technology, we come to understand and love each other more by sharing stories of our human condition. Of course, this being Earth we continue to endure suffering, but know that in the end, this drives us collectively toward our ultimate goal.

I myself have engaged in heated debate over issues like gun control, immigration and the like, but I've had to remind myself these are all opportunities for growth. It's far less about individual issues than how we treat each other, despite our differing opinions. If you at all want to rid yourself and humanity of suffering, the best thing you can do is to practice love. It's important for everyone to remember that we *choose* to come to Earth precisely to encounter challenges. By doing so, we accelerate the pace and depth of our learning. It's similar to learning something by doing it, rather than reading about it. So remember to treat your adversaries with the utmost kindness and respect.

Knowing that reincarnation is truly a part of our existence, our souls must go somewhere in between lives. I'm confident we go to Heaven. I believe however, that we go to different levels of Heaven based on the development of one's individual soul. Hindus, Buddhists and NDErs hold this belief in common as well, though descriptions of Heaven vary greatly even among individuals of the same background. This is analogous to the joke about the three blind men who are asked to describe an elephant. One says it is like a snake, as he holds its tail. Another says it's like a tree, as he hugs its leg. The third says it's like a sail, as he waves the ear back and forth. Obviously, they are each experiencing a different aspect of the animal. Whether one defines Heaven in the traditional sense, or sees it as comprised of levels or realms, something beyond this world does exist.

The good news is that all of us will get there and be provided a respite from the turmoil of earthly existence. Eventually, we will be free of suffering once and for all. As my angels told me, "Suffering isn't going to last forever." Taken with the messages of my STEs, it's clear that not one soul will be lost. We are one with God and cannot be separated. We continue learning through many lifetimes until we reach the pinnacle of Heaven, the Kingdom of God, which is a return to pure love.

Until then there are habits we can adopt to help make our time on Earth as pleasant as possible and move us along on our spiritual trajectory. Based on my experiences, I've outlined below four practices that everyone can take up, that add up to LOVE:

Look for God in Everyone
Look past individual personas to that which is God within everyone. In some, the light is harder to see than in others, but it is there. The more we recognize it in each other, the brighter our lights shine. Treat everyone with the reverence with which you would treat God, for he or she is also God.

Optimize Suffering
Do not get lost in your grief or pain, but instead learn from your suffering—it is a gift that will not last forever. Examine negative feelings and work on transforming them into positive, loving thoughts and actions. This is what leads to healing not only of the body, but of your soul and that of all souls, the collective *one*.

Value Gifts of the Spirit
Do not dismiss coincidences as merely such. They are gifts to keep you aligned with your life's purpose. Once you are open to these, you become aware of your other God-given gifts. Claim your inherited right to truth, knowledge, and wisdom through development of your gifts of prophesy (precognition), clairvoyance (clear vision), clairaudience (clear hearing), and clairsentience (clear feeling), etc. There are many books, classes and more to teach you how.

Engage God
All souls are working toward reuniting with God. It is in the awareness of oneness that we move closer to unity. As such, selfless remediation through prayer, meditation and service to others are the best ways to engage God. Like the prodigal son, we see our father over the horizon as we make our way home. We hear his voice, dim and distant, but ever-more clear the closer we get.

When you practice these habits, you are learning love and teaching it to others in the process. Love is the only thing we take with us after death, and it is truly the only thing that exists!

Afterword

Sharing My Story

I n the first few years after my STEs I grappled with what I was supposed to do with them, if anything. Were they for me only or was I to tell others, and if so, whom? On one hand, the messages were given directly to me. Had God intended it to be a confidential conversation? On the other hand, I realized the information I received had profound implications for humanity. It was hard to ignore the inner voice urging me to share my testimony. Was this the calling to which Pastor Gillespie alluded?

For a while I tried to ignore it, aware that putting myself out there publicly invited scrutiny. I knew I was not alone, though. A vast amount of literature exists by those who have chosen to tell about their STEs and NDEs, often risking careers and enduring backlash from peers, family, and friends. Their experiences, like mine, must have been so compelling that keeping it to themselves was ultimately not an option. For this I'm grateful because the collective body of work by experiencers is instrumental to the spiritual evolution of humankind. The more we share, the more quickly we arrive at the same conclusion of oneness and the love inherent in our identity.

Still, in the beginning I considered that perhaps my experiences were too sacred to share. I tossed and turned many nights wondering what God wanted me to do. The answer finally came in the form of a mystical interlude after praying for direction and drifting off to sleep one evening.

I was awakened by soft music coming from my iPhone, which I laid on my nightstand next to my bed every night. I puzzled at how the music had started suddenly playing on its own. My phone had never done *that* before. I typically don't set an alarm, but when I do it emits a loud, high-pitched *ping-ping-ping* to ensure I don't fall back to sleep. This was unmistakably music. I focused on the words, then realized God was speaking to me again, this time through song:

Why me Lord? What have I ever done to deserve even one of the blessings I've known? Why me Lord? What did I ever do that was worth love from you and the kindness you've shown?

Try me Lord, if you think there's a way that I can repay what I've taken from you. Maybe Lord, I can show someone else what I've been through myself on my way back to you.

Lord help me Jesus, I've wasted it, so help me Jesus, I know what I am. Now that I know that I've needed you, so help me, Jesus, my soul's in your hand.

I felt that familiar lump in my throat as another song started; *I Did It My Way*. As I rolled over to grab my phone, the music stopped. Scrolling through a few screens, I saw no apps were open, particularly my music player. I laid back down hoping the music would start again, but it didn't and I dozed off.

In the morning I searched my music library not knowing if either song was part of my collection. I often download an entire album for a few titles to add to a playlist, then forget about the rest. I wouldn't have purposely added *I Did it My Way* to my library; it wasn't in my wheel house, as Bailey would put it. I did find an Elvis version, but I'm certain it had not been Elvis' distinctive voice I'd heard the night before. I double and triple-checked my library, but the Elvis version was the only one I owned.

A quick check proved that *Why Me* was not in my library, either. I'd heard the song before but was barely familiar with it. Growing up, the radio at our house was usually tuned-in to country music and I'd probably heard it back then. I searched the internet and found that Kris Kristofferson had written it and it was a hit on both the country and pop charts in the seventies.

Neither song was obscure, but I'd never purposely listened to either. Taken together, the message became clear to me:

I can do whatever I want, for we have free will (*I did it my way*), but it would be pleasing to God (*the kindness you've shown … I can repay*) if I used the gift of writing that he's given me and not waste it (*I've wasted it*) to share my story (*what I've been through*

158

myself) and be a part of this great awakening that is revealing to mankind who we really are, our connection to God, and our destiny (*on my way back to you*).

God wanted me to share my story, and in fact it would be a waste if I didn't. The next day I formulated an outline for this book. I believe if you're reading it now, God is directing you onto a new path of discovery, too.

Since I didn't know how long it would take to write a book, I looked for a professional outlet that would allow me to begin verbally sharing the truths that had been revealed to me. When I found the International Association for Near-Death Studies on the internet, I found my family of kindred spirits! The messages being brought back with experiencers aligned perfectly with those I'd been given. Additionally, the organization is devoted to scientific research and counts highly respected medical professionals, researchers and other credentialed scientists among its members. This was a group on the frontier of a revolution bringing science and spirituality back together. I'd found my outlet.

It was August 2017 when I first shared my story publicly. I had filled out a Speaker's Proposal Form to tell my story at the IANDS national conference in Denver that year, but I didn't expect to hear back from them because: 1) Their focus is on the near-death experience, and I had *not* died; and 2) I was an unknown in the spiritual community—I had no book, articles, interviews or other presentations of which to speak. Luckily for me, there were others who proposed to speak about their STEs and IANDS put us together on their first STE panel.

I was thrilled, but I would have to work hard to whittle down my story; it took nearly two hours every time I told it privately. Whenever I sat down to formulate an abridged version however, I became frustrated because there was so much to tell. Leaving anything out seemed sacrilegious to me. Even as I write this book, the same is true. It has been frustrating to cut other miraculous things that have occurred to me, but they simply didn't fit within the scope of my core experiences. I guess that's why authors tend to write more than one book (hint, hint)!

I let my conference preparation slide and before I knew it, my stepdaughter had arrived from the Netherlands for a visit. Danique was in New Jersey for three weeks, and her visit was priceless because it was few and far between that we had such opportunity. Instead of preparing, I opted for carefree days at the beach, lunches out and lots of shopping with Danique—and, oh boy, did we have fun!

Before I knew it, the conference was only two days away. Danique and I managed to pull together a poster I committed to displaying, but I still had not touched my presentation. It came down to the wire and the only time I had left was during the Thursday flight from New Jersey to Colorado where the IANDS Conference would be held. I barely scrawled out an outline before the plane landed. As we touched down, I pressed my forehead against the window hoping the coolness of the rain trickling down the outside pane would relieve an oncoming headache. Nerves.

At the hotel I unpacked my bags, unzipped the pretty purple and yellow tote bag with the big IANDS logo on it, and sifted through the literature until I found the conference schedule. Yup, there I was, listed as a panelist for the Friday three o'clock presentation. My eyes shifted a column further to "Room Location," and I discovered the STE Panel was to take place in the main lecture hall—also the largest. I swallowed hard. For the first time, I was going to tell a room full of strangers that God spoke to me—and then, *what I was told*—aye! Though I knew my audience was like-minded, it's still daunting to step out of the spiritual closet, so-to-speak.

Being an attendee as well as a speaker, my schedule was filled from the time I arrived to the time I departed. The lecture rooms, halls and vendor areas in the stately hotel buzzed with energy. I was quickly caught up in the positive vibe and my worry dissolved. I spent what little free time I had between lectures and workshops meeting fascinating people. Lunch and dinner afforded even greater opportunity to sit one-on-one and hear others' amazing stories in-depth. I completely gave up on the idea of polishing my presentation—or more appropriately, sanding it down with 1,200-grit sandpaper to fit within the allotted time.

Friday morning passed in the blink of an eye. I'd managed to keep my mind off my talk until I spotted my co-panelist Bruce, in the hallway. When I approached him and his wife at the conference to say hello, the first thing he asked was if I was ready.

I feigned a polite smile. "As ready as I'll ever be."

Half-an-hour before the presentation, I stepped onto the elevator and headed to my room for a few deep breaths and to review my notes. I second guessed my content. *Did I omit the wrong things? Should I take out something else instead?* In a moment of despair, I decided I couldn't rely on myself. I prayed, asking God to give me the words he wanted people to hear, adding as an afterthought, "All within twenty minutes, *please.*"

I made my way downstairs and though I had used the bathroom already and didn't need to stop, I felt compelled to make a right turn into the Ladies Room before entering the lecture hall. To my horror my skirt was hiked up in back, the outer swath of lace caught in the zipper! Crisis averted. I offered up a quick thanks and departed the restroom.

Tech guys were running around the lecture hall doing sound checks and playing with lighting at the back of the room. As my nerves ratcheted up a notch, I reminded myself that I'd once routinely spoken in front of audiences during the heyday of my career.

I joined Bruce, the other panelist, and our moderator on stage. The third panelist had bowed out and that gave each of us a little more time. The table and chairs were set up as I'd seen them for other panelists. I'd visualized presenting in the same way, seated at the table with a microphone in front of me. I made mental notes to sit up straight, talk into the mic, cross legs at ankles, don't rest on my elbows, etc.

As I sat down, however, Bruce leaned over and whispered that he would present standing up with the mic stand only and no podium, and he would go first. *Aye!* A look of surprise must have come over my face because he immediately added that I didn't have to stand because he'd chosen to do so.

"No, I'll stand too," I muttered, not wanting to interrupt the dynamics of the overall presentation.

Bruce began and stopped at precisely the right time, then handed the mic to our moderator to introduce me. His presentation had flowed like a beautiful river and the audience was captivated.

My heart raced as I maneuvered out of my seat and positioned myself on stage. I took a deep breath, then something unexpected happened. A peaceful easiness fell over me like a veil and I immediately felt tuned-in to the audience. An unplanned joke about being Italian, juxtaposing Bruce's laid-back style with my, let's say enthusiasm, came out of nowhere, and I was out of the gate.

I told my story as it had happened and relayed the important messages God had given me four years earlier. Passion overwhelmed me at one point and my voice cracked, but I did not lose composure. My presentation was seamless, and I fit all the main points in during the allotted time. God once again had my back.

People were moved by the experiences Bruce and I shared with them. We had to be shooed out of the lecture hall along with a small crowd to continue our Q&A in the hallway. Many people came to me throughout the conference asking for more details, which I happily obliged utilizing the presentation board Danique and I had created. Several attendees told me it was one of their favorite presentations because it provided a different but corroborative account of the messages being brought back by near-death experiencers.

Interestingly, a couple in their late fifties approached me and said they were shocked when I divulged my past life as Absalom. The husband, they explained, uses "Absalom" as his computer and internet go-to password, but has no idea why—it was something he'd picked at random. I was certain the synchronicity was a gift to us all; for them, a message they were meant to hear, and for me, validation that my story is meant to be heard.

I will keep speaking to audiences about my STEs and revealing what I learn as I continue to evolve. Much has happened in the ensuing years, most notably I have had incidents of spontaneous mediumship and channeled writing. I am practicing the four habits of L.O.V.E. and allowing spirit to guide my path. It is indeed a miraculous journey!

PHOTOS

My clan near the Cliffs of Moher, Ireland, a place to which my spiritual journey unexpectedly diverted me. Left to right: Eric, Bailey, Danique, Jasper and me. (Photo by permission, Kat Rolland)

Me (left) with the tapestry at Bunratty Castle in County Clare, Ireland, hanging above. The "professor" identified this as depicting the life of Absalom. It is the scene where David is given the news of Absalom's death.

Lord Fredric Leighton's "David," depicting King David looking out over the gates of Jerusalem, distraught upon learning of the death of Absalom. Permanent display, The Cleveland Museum of Art. (Photo by permission, The Cleveland Museum of Art)

Personal postcards purchased at The Cleveland Museum of Art (Lord Fredric Leighton's "David"), and at Bunratty Castle, County Clare, Ireland.

The day we renewed our wedding vows. Eric looks
pretty good for just having had a "rood" canal!

Charlie, our sweet Cairn Terrier
whose ears never up and was my
constant writing companion. Rest in
peace, baby boy.

Me in the Kidron Valley with what was thought to be Absalom's Pillar until modern dating techniques proved otherwise.

In 2017, Eric and I went to Jerusalem for my 50th birthday. Absalom would have spent many days at the sites I visited. I felt some familiarity, but I cannot say it was memory.

Interestingly, my randomly chosen guide told me Absalom was her favorite biblical person, herself being a rebellious spirit. Also, her friend was writing a book about the very obscure Tamar (Absalom's sister). I hadn't told her a thing about my experiences! What are the chances? Eventually I did tell her, and she was amazed!

Standing in front of King David's currently-under-excavation palace in the City of David, Jerusalem in 2017, five years after my STEs.

At the Garden of Gethsemane.

Learning about Buddhism during a
visit to The Big Buddha, Phuket, Thai-
land, 2018.

Bibliography & Suggested Reading

Nancy's true short story, "Ladybugs and Hummingbirds," about further mystical encounters with her mother, can be found in Emily Rodavich's book, Mystical Interludes II (listed in the bibliography below).

Aldridge, Faye. *Real Messages from Heaven, and Other True Stories of Miracles, Divine Intervention & Supernatural Occurrences.* Shippensburg, PA: Destiny Image Publishers, 2011.

Alexander, Eben, M.D. *Proof of Heaven. A Neurosurgeon's Journey into the Afterlife.* New York: Simon & Schuster, 2012.

———. *The Map of Heaven. How Science, Religion, and Ordinary People are Proving the Afterlife.* New York: Simon & Schuster,

——— and Karen Newell. *Living in a Mindful Universe. A Neurosurgeon's Journey into the Heart of Consciousness.* U.S.A.: Rodale Wellness, 2017.

Atwater, P.M.H. *Beyond the Light. What isn't Being Said About the Near-Death Experience.* New York: Birch Lane Press, 1994.

———. *Near-Death Experiences, The Rest of the Story.* Charlottesville, VA: Hampton Roads Publishing Company, Inc., 2011.

Baden, Joel. *The Historical David. The Real Life of an Invented Hero.* New York: Harper One, 2014.

Blackaby, Henry and Richard, and Claude King. *Experiencing God. Knowing and Doing the Will of God.* Nashville: B&H Publishing Group, 2008.

Brinkley, Dannion. *Saved by the Light. The True Story of a Man who Died Twice and the Profound Revelations He Received.* New York: Harper Collins, 2018

Burke, John. *Imagine Heaven. Near-Death Experiences, God's Promises, and the Exhilarating Future That Awaits You.* Grand Rapids, MI: Baker Books, 2015.

Byrne, Lorna. *Angels in My Hair.* New York: Penguin Random House, 2008.

Cannon, Dolores. *Jesus and the Essenes.* Huntsville, AL: Ozark Mountain Publishing, 1992.

———. They Walked with Jesus. Huntsville, AL: Ozark Mountain Publishing, 1994.

Chopra, Deepak, M.D. and Menas Kafatos, Ph.D. *You Are the Universe. Discovering Your Cosmic Self and Why It Matters.* New York: Harmony Books, 2017.

Church, W.H. *Edgar Cayce's Story of the Soul.* Virginia Beach: The Association for Research and Enlightenment, Inc., 1989.

Clark, Nancy. *Revelations from the Light: What I Learned About Life's Purposes.* Fairfield, IL: First World Publishing, 2017.

Cohen, Doris Eliana, PH.D. *Dreaming on Both Sides of the Brain. Discover the Secret Language of the Night.* Charlottesville, VA: Hampton Roads Publishing, Inc., 2017.

———. Repetition. Past Lives, Life, and Rebirth. New York: Hay House, 2008.

Colbert, Moses U. *The Bible and the Near Death Experience*. Portland, OR: BookBaby, 2013

Dossey, Larry, M.D. *One Mind. How Our Individual Mind is Part of a Greater Consciousness and Why it Matters*. Carlsbad, CA: Hay House, Inc., 2013.

Doyle, Tom. *Dreams and Visions. Is Jesus Awakening the Muslim World?* Nashville: W Publishing Group, 2012.

Galland, Leo, M.D. *Already Here. A Doctor Discovers the Truth about Heaven*. Carlsbad, CA: Hay House, Inc., 2018.

Hanh, Thich Nhat. *The Heart of the Buddha's Teaching. Transforming Suffering into Peace, Joy, and Liberation*. New York: Harmony Books, 2015.

Hill, Roy L., Psy.D. *Jesus and the Near-Death Experience*. Hova, U.K.: White Crow Books, 2017.

Holdaway, David. *They Saw Jesus. Modern Day Face to Face Encounters with Jesus Christ*. Life Publications, 2007

Jackson, Laura Lynne. *The Light Between Us. Stories from Heaven. Lessons for the Living*. New York: Spiegel & Grau, 2015

Lipton, Bruce H., Ph.D., *The Biology of Belief. Unleashing the Power of Consciousness, Matter & Miracles*. Carlsbad, CA: Hay House, Inc., 2005.

Long, Jeffrey, M.D. and Paul Perry. *Evidence of the Afterlife. The Science of Near-Death Experiences*. U.S.A.: Harper Collins, 2010.

Moody, Raymod A., M.D. *Life After Life (with new forword by Eben Alexander, M.D.)*. New York: Harper One, 2015.

Moorjani, Anita. *Dying to Be Me. My Journey from Cancer, To Near Death, to True Healing*. Carlsbad, CA: Hay House, 2012.

————. *What if This is Heaven? How Our Cultural Myths Prevent Us from Experiencing Heaven on Earth.* Carlsbad, CA: Hay House, 2016.

Neal, Mary C., M.D. *To Heaven and Back: A Doctor's Extraordinary Account of Her Death, Heaven, Angels, and Life Again.* Colorado Springs, CO: WaterBrook Press, 2012.

Newton, Michael, Ph.D. *Memories of the Afterlife. Life Between Lives. Stories of Personal Transformation.* Woodbury, MN: Llewellyn Publications, 2015.

Olsen, Jeff. *I Knew Their Hearts. The Amazing True Story of a Journey Beyond the Veil to Learn the Silent Language of the Heart.* Springville, UT: Plain Sight Publishing, 2012.

Parti, Rajiv, M.D. *Dying to Wake Up. A Doctor's Voyage into the Afterlife and the Wisdom He Brought Back.* New York: Atria Books, 2016.

Prophet, Elizabeth Clare. *Reincarnation. The Missing Link in Christianity.* Corwin Springs, MT: Summit University Press, 1997.

Puryear, Herbert Bruce. *Why Jesus Taught Reincarnation. A Better News Gospel.* Scottsdale, AZ: New Paradigm Press, 1992.

Qureshi, Nabeel. *Seeking Allah, Finding Jesus (with foreword by Lee Strobel).* Grand Rapids, MI: Zondervan, 2014.

Robbins, Jim. *The Man Who Planted Trees. A Story of Lost Groves. The Science of Trees, and a Plan to Save the Planet.* New York: Spiegel & Grau, 2015.

Rodavich, Emily. *Mystical Interludes. An Ordinary Person's Extraordinary Experiences.* Boca Raton, FL.: Citrine Publishing, 2016.

————. *Mystical Interludes II. A Collection of Ordinary People's Mystical Experiences.* Asheville, NC: Citrine Publishing, 2018.

Rogers, Sandra. *Lessons from the Light. Insights from a Journey to the Other Side.* Grand Rapids, MI: Grand Central Publishing, 2009.

Rynes, Nancy. *Awakenings from the Light. 12 Life Lessons from a Near Death Experience.* Denver: Solace Press, 2015.

Semikew, Walter, M.D. *Born Again. Reincarnation Cases Involving Evidence of Past Lives, with Xenoglossy Cases Researched by Ian Stevenson, MD.* 2012, ISBN 978-0-9662982-4-6 (no other information available)

Stavish, Mark. *Between the Gates. Lucid Dreaming, Astral Projection, and the Body of Light in Western Esotericism.* San Francisco, CA: Red Whell/Weiser, LLC, 2008.

Storm, Howard. *My Descent into Death. A Second Chance at Life.* New York: Doubleday, 2005.

Taylor, Jill Bolte, Ph.D. *My Stroke of Insight. A Brain Scientist's Personal Journey.* New York: Plume, 2009.

Todeschi, Kevin J. *Edgar Cayce on the Reincarnation of Biblical Characters.* Virginia Beach: The Association for Research and Enlightenment, Inc., 1999.

Tolle, Eckhart. *The Power of Now. A Guide to Spiritual Enlightenment.* Novato, CA: New World Library, 1999.

Tompkins, Ptolemy and Tyler Beddoes. *Proof of Angels.* New York: Howard Books, 2016.

Weiss, Brian L., M.D. *Many Lives, Many Masters.* New York: Simon & Schuster, Inc., 1988.

Woollacott, Marjorie Hines. *Infinite Awareness. The Awakening of a Scientific Mind.* Lanham, MD: Rowman & Littlefield, 2015.

ABOUT THE AUTHOR

Nancy van Alphen grew up in a middle-class family in rural-suburban northeast Ohio, where she lived most of her life. Currently, she and her husband Eric live in southern New Jersey (or *South Jersey* as the locals call it), minutes outside of Philadelphia. She regularly makes the eight hour drive back to Ohio to visit family and friends. While blessed to have had a series of divine, spiritually transformative experiences, she considers herself "pretty ordinary—for the most part."

Not as ordinary is her family life. With children living on both sides of the pond, and a husband who travels extensively between several continents for work, she manages her life around time zones and flight schedules. Eric is a native of Holland, where his children, Jasper and Danique still reside. Danique is a graphic designer and provided the cover art and layout for *Caught Between Heaven & Earth*. Nancy's daughter, Bailey, resides in Ohio. Charlie, the family's Cairn terrier whose ears never went up, recently passed on, but is loved and missed by all.

A seasoned traveler, Nancy has visited Jerusalem seeking connection with her past life as Absalom and that of his father, King David. She relates in *Caught Between Heaven & Earth*, her travel to Ireland, which is significant to her story. She has also traveled to Paris, Rome, London, Bangkok, Amsterdam, and a host of other locations throughout the U.S. and Europe. She loves travel, but hates packing.

A graduate of Oberlin College, Nancy majored in cultural anthropology with a keen interest in archaeology. She subscribed to Darwinian evolution, as was common in her field, but knew even then as an agnostic that it was purely materialistic science.

Nancy began writing as a journalism major at Lorain County Community College, where she was editor of the newspaper for two years before obtaining her associate degree. During her time at Oberlin College, she worked as copy editor for the regional daily newspaper, *The Chronicle Telegram*.

Writing segued into a marketing career where Nancy first worked as a copywriter on the Cleveland advertising scene. She quickly developed skills as a marketing strategist and has held positions with companies of all sizes, working on both national and international accounts. She remembers most fondly being part of an education sales team for Apple Computer, managing marketing activities and tradeshows during a time that buzzed with excitement over each new technology release. She currently works as an independent marketing consultant and includes her husband's employer among her clients. Joining him at tradeshows and swanky after-parties in Las Vegas is "just part of the job," she says.

Semi-retired, Nancy is heavily involved in volunteer work with IANDS (International Association for Near-Death Studies) and is busy establishing a local group in Philadelphia. She has been a hospice volunteer for the past four years and has been a big sister in the Big Brothers/Big Sisters program. Her hobbies include travel, reading, snorkeling, cooking, and exploration of all things spiritual.

Nancy offers presentations about her experiences and spirituality to interested groups. For more information visit www. NancyVanAlphen.com.